D1563053

TELLING THE TRUTH

The Groundbreaking Articles that Saved West Coast Swing

KATHERINE EASTVOLD

Complete Collection with Brand New & Expanded Material

During times of universal deceit,
telling the truth becomes a revolutionary act.

-George Orwell

To my husband Nick,
with whom I have seen the best of times and the worst of times.

To the One above,
who let me write about dance first.

And to my readers across the globe…
You amaze me.
Thank you.

CONTENTS

Introduction

Before We Begin
What West Coast Swing is, and More...

I began writing for the West Coast Swing (WCS) community almost two years ago. My first article, *The Nissy*, was a huge success. It had nearly 3,000 online hits in the first 48 hours. Feedback poured in from all over the world. It was amazing, humbling and a little overwhelming. I clearly struck a nerve. For everyone.

Though written for the WCS community, I heard from Salsa dancers, Tango dancers, ballroom studio owners and fine arts enthusiasts... and this trend of reaching outside communities continued the more I wrote. By now my readership is huge, and I estimate that nearly 25% of my readers worldwide are those who have never danced a step of WCS. But they are still avid readers.

I cannot pinpoint why this is. I have heard it's because I am an amazing writer (that is still sinking in... thank you!), because I have put words to what people have been thinking in their work, home and personal lives and because somehow, some way, my words give people courage. I don't know how all of that is possible when I'm writing to the tortured souls of our small little WCS community, but I'm not complaining.

I do write to set people free. I do hope to give people courage. I do listen to everything I'm sent, told and written... I care about my readers, I care about people and I care about the truth. So whether you are a WCS dancer or not, I welcome you, and hope you gain some insight, hope and joy into your own lives, wherever they may be.

So. What exactly *is* West Coast Swing?

To put it simply, WCS is a swing dance that originated, like all the other swing dances of the world, in the American music movement of the 1930's, also called swing. This new music took the world by storm, and dancers everywhere started developing a new dance to do with their dance buddies and friends which fit this new genre of music.

Not surprisingly, each region came up with their own "style" or "version" of this new dance. It's why we hear so many different terms for swing dancing: Jitterbug, East Coast Swing, Lindy Hop, Smooth Lindy, etc. etc. It's also why we hear so many different versions of how the dance was born. We are so lucky to have so many of those first dancers still with us today, but not one of them will tell you the same story about how swing dancing was born.

What is very clear is that by the time the 1950's hit, there had been great efforts by studios, teachers and dancers to define and name each of the versions of swing out there. Since swing dancing was born on the social dance floors (such dances are often known as "street" dances), there was, and still is, some great resistance from the dancers who were there when it was created. Artists don't usually like labels, and thus there has always been some argument as to when it was and where it was and how it was each swing dance started. Shoot. They even debate whether or not there even *are* different styles!

But I really don't care. I'm just glad it started. And I'm incredibly glad I found it.

I fell in love with East Coast Swing first, dancing 'til I dropped at the famous Derby in Hollywood before Big Bad Voodoo Daddy blew up and the re-birth of swing hit the nation in the early 1990's. But when I went home for the summer, ECS was no where to be found. I was surrounded by nothing but ballroom studios and country western bars. And so I went there.

Now, you have to know that I grew up a dancer. I loved jazz classes, hated ballet classes and went to the local cotillion classes and always made it to the partner dance finals without ever taking a lick of ballroom lessons. I know now that I was born with the "follower" gene. If a guy knew how to lead, I could follow. From the get go. I was so lucky, and I didn't even know it yet.

But then I tried WCS. It was a staple at the country bars and WCS classes had begun at some of the local ballroom studios. I remember it really well because, well, I thought the dance was ridiculous. It made no sense. Growing up in dance classes, I had 'a 5-6-7-8!' pounded into my head, but now this crazy dance wanted me to only take 6 beats? And start a new pattern before the 7,8???

I was floored. It drove me nuts. It made me work. I couldn't just "follow" my way through this dance. I needed to know the rules.

And then I attended my first WCS convention. They didn't play country western music (which for me, at the time, was a super big plus…), but more importantly, the dancers were phenomenal. I mean, every single woman was completely different and yet, absolutely amazing. The men too. I could watch them dance all night long, and go home knowing that there was no way in hell I would ever get to look that good.

Oh my, if I only knew.

When I returned to UCLA, I took buses, I hitched rides and I sat on people's laps in packed cars… I did everything I could to make it to any WCS class I could. And to attend every WCS dance possible. I learned on the floor, and I learned from amazing teachers. I split private lessons and I took a million notes. I learned and I learned and I learned.

And quite frankly, almost 20 years later, I never, ever, ever became bored. I went on to become a WCS champion and I even opened my own studio. I've taught at nearly every single WCS venue in the state of California and I met my husband while teaching him WCS.

I am a smart cookie. I graduated from UCLA with honors. But I never tired of WCS, and here's why.

RULES OF WEST COAST SWING

If you've ever taken a partner dance class, like Salsa or Waltz, you'll remember that there is always a basic step. One basic step. Oh, there are other steps too, built on that one basic, but if you had to, you could do that one basic step all night long and have it nailed down pat after a while.

And whatever the rhythms of that basic step were, say "quick-quick, slow, slow" or "slow, quick-quick, slow, quick-quick," then almost all the steps you learned afterwards were exactly the same, just in different directions. If you've ever learned East Coast Swing, let's say the single rhythm version (step – step –

rock step), then you might remember that every single turn, every head loop, every spin you spun... you were still dancing "step – step – rock step." Never changed.

But WCS? Ohhhh no. No, no, no, no no. There isn't one basic step. There are EIGHT! And that, my dears, is still in debate among some circles. I've found a teacher who names six basics and I've seen another teacher who says there are 22 basics! But it really doesn't matter. WCS has more than one basic. And that's what matters.

What's even worse (or better!) is that when you count out these eight basic patterns, you'll discover that they are all different lengths. That's right. The Starter Step is only 4 counts long. The Whip is 8 counts long. All the rest are 6 counts long.

Oh, the glorious dance of WCS! How I love it! How amazing it truly is. Oh, how it does stand out against the stark grey background of the million partner and street dances done across the globe. The dance of WCS isn't easy to learn. But it sure is worth it.

Because, as you may already have guessed, the more complicated a dance is, the further it can go. The more it can do. The greater it can change. It's magnificent.

Here are the eight basics of WCS:

-The Push Break	-The Starter Step
-The Left Side Pass	-The Tuck Out
-The Right Side Pass	-The Tuck
-The Underarm Turn	-The Whip

Some schools of thought include more basics, like the Throw Out or the Turning Basic. Some include less. But the fact remains that we all agree there is much more than one basic, and if you want to dance WCS with no matter who or where you go, you'll need the above 8 to dance it successfully.

THE RHYTHMS

This is not of the utmost importance, but it wouldn't be fair to allow you to continue on without at least giving you a basic understanding of rhythms. You're going to hear me talk about rhythms every once in a while, and a lot of teachers throw out the terminology in class but don't take the time to break down what it means for you.

So, if you'll permit me, let me give you a brief definition / explanation of what rhythms are and what they mean. If you really don't care, just skip on by to the next heading.

Basically, the term "rhythm" refers to two beats of music. If you've taken a jazz or hip hop class where the choreography is broken down into sets of 8, then that set of 8 has four rhythms to it. We don't really use the term rhythm in jazz or hip hop though, because rhythm also refers to the amount of steps taken during those two beats of music.

In jazz and hip hop, we're not always transferring weight on every beat. We're doing arm movements, or knee pops, etc etc. But in partner dancing? In partner dancing almost everything we call out refers to a step being made. Since we're dancing with a partner, it's kind of important that we all transfer our weight at the same time, lest one of us gets stepped on. As such, you will most often hear the term "rhythm" in partner dance classes.

So. What kinds of rhythms are there? In general, there are single, double and triple rhythms. That's all you really need to know for this book and for most dance classes world wide. Single rhythm, double rhythm, triple rhythm and you're done.

Now, if you've been tracking with me so far, you'll probably already guess what the difference is between these three. In a single rhythm, you take one step. You transfer your weight once during two beats of music. In a double rhythm, you step twice during two beats of music (aka walking to the beat). In a triple rhythm... yep, you guessed it, you take three steps during two beats of music.

It is really popular for teachers to use the words "slow" to refer to a single rhythm and "quick-quick" to refer to a double rhythm. If you've ever taken a ballroom or social dance class, you might have learned all the dances in quicks and slows only. That's understandable. Almost all the dances are comprised of single and double rhythms.

Except for swing. Swing dancing is where you fall upon triple rhythms. And I mean, a lot of triple rhythms. As I'm sure you can guess, doing a triple rhythm is much harder than doing a double rhythm and much MUCH harder than doing a single rhythm. But once you get the hang of it, it's a lot of fun.

Since East Coast Swing is the most popular swing dance taught worldwide, you might have already heard the terms single rhythm and triple rhythm and you just didn't know it. Remember that "step – step – rock step" I mentioned earlier when talking about ECS? A lot of dance instructors call that "Single Rhythm Swing." That's because the first two rhythms of this 6 count pattern are single rhythms. "Step – Step" is just code for "single – single."

Once you've mastered this step pattern, the teacher will move you into the advanced version, or Triple Rhythm Swing. Your slow steps at the beginning will now suddenly go much faster: "step, step, step" to one side, then "step, step, step" to the other side, and then comes the rock step again, a nice double rhythm that suddenly feels like *that's* the slow part of each pattern. Those "step, step, step"s are really just triple rhythms. The basic step for Single Rhythm Swing and the basic step for Triple Rhythm Swing are exactly the same in length. They are each three rhythms long, which means they are each 6 beats long.

Ta da! I hope you stayed with me there. If not, come back to it later. You'll catch on.

What do you mean by "Telling the Truth"?

Now we get down to the heart and soul of it: why I started writing, and why this book is even necessary.

Look. The world has changed dramatically in the last 15 years. A large part of that is due to the internet, the abolishment of analog and non-digital formats (read: historical records) and an even larger part of it is due to social networking and instant communications, like texting. My little community of WCS has changed dramatically because of Narcissism, addiction, YouTube and an ugly little political system that's supported the monopoly of a few and destroyed the progress, joy and training of the majority. This includes newcomers, veteran dancers and longtime legends of the dance.

This, along with reasons I outline in my writing, has spawned not only a corrupt hierarchy, but it's also created a completely different dance. And I do mean, completely different.

As such, dancers were getting hurt. Badly.

It's bad enough that such an amazing dance was brought to the brink of extinction just because of a few egos and pockets, but it was worse to watch and listen as every level of dancer was caught in wake of such behavior, and suffering damage physically, mentally and financially.

Some tried to speak up. Many talked in hushed whispers. Even more left the dance. But ultimately, no one did anything. We all saw it, but we never said it.

Not publicly.

So I did. And have paid quite the price.

Thankfully, the reward has been the renewal of real WCS and the empowerment of dancers and teachers world wide. There is nothing more fulfilling than hearing from all corners of the globe that teachers and students alike are trusting their own internal instincts again, instead of only trusting others who never intended to do more than rob them of their dignity, strength and money.

I never expected my writing to empower readers outside of dancing, but still, I receive so many stories that go far beyond any dance floor. So when all is said and done, the cost may have been great on my part, but the reward has been greater.

I hope you find more than what you are looking for in this book, and in my books to come.

With love, passion and gratitude,

Katherine Eastvold

The Articles

When I started teaching my SwingIN!s in January of 2011, which you will soon read about, I handed out folders filled with articles and outlines to supplement the subjects I was teaching on.

I soon learned how valuable these handouts were, and started writing, printing and releasing them at conventions, my workshops and classes and, more importantly, online.

The following are the articles I wrote for public consumption in the order they were released.

Monday, April 4th 2011

The Nissy
What I Could Do Without

"Nissy" is my nickname for the Narcissists of our dance community. It can be yours too. It's high time we had one.

Narcissism has increased at an alarming rate these last 10 years in our dance community, and the damage has been far reaching. As such, it's important that we who love the dance family become aware of the behavior and its effects. When we do, we can protect ourselves, the joy of our dancing and the joy of others when they are struggling and confused.

So what exactly IS a Narcissist? To put it very simply, it's someone who is ruled by "egotism, vanity, conceit, or simple selfishness." Though glamorized in the movies and on TV, the Narcissistic Personality Disorder (NPD) is a social disorder that's extremely destructive, especially in the lives of those that surround them. Because a Narcissist is incapable of putting anyone's needs before their own. Because they only see others as a means to meet their needs and boost their ego/image, their presence comes at a great cost to those in their family, workplace and community. Our community.

Now, do I think every dance scene in the world is flooded with full blown NPD's? No. Not worldwide. But I can bear witness to a number of communities with 50% or more of the people being Nissies. And that number is growing fast for two reasons. First, Nissies tend to attract other Nissies to the dance. They often form a group, known as elitism. Secondly, those who used to have healthy personalities have come to believe that they must mimic Narcissistic behavior in order to be accepted, to win, to be admired, and to be danced with. It's time we admitted the problem, acknowledge the behavior and take action to protect ourselves accordingly, because good partner dancing, amazing partner dancing... worthwhile partner dancing... can never ever be done by a Nissy.

If you Google Narcissism, you'll find a list of traits on a number of websites: *'haughty body language', 'exaggerates their accomplishments,' 'uses people without considering what it will cost them', 'flatters and enjoys the company of those that admire them, but detests, belittles or ignores those who do not'*, etc., etc. But one Narcissist is not like the other.

The textbook type of Narcissist is what they call an "exhibitionist," but there are many other types of Narcissists, including "aggressive," "elitist," and even "sexual." The list is quite extensive. Not all are alike and they aren't always easy to identify, because they are rarely rude in the beginning. They can be charming, charismatic and flirtatious, and others are quiet, reserved or even awkward.

So how can you identify Narcissism in our dance community?

In her book, "*Why is it Always About You?: The Seven Deadly Sins of Narcissism*," Sandy Hotchkiss outlines the "deadly sins" a

Narcissist will commit. These "deadly sins" have found their way onto our social dance floors, into our workshops, our private lessons and our competitions. I'm sure you'll think of a dancer (or two, or three, and depending on where you live, a whole lot more!) when you read through these characteristics and examples:

- **ARROGANCE:** A Nissy who is feeling deflated tends to re-inflate by diminishing, debasing or degrading somebody else. Example: They didn't make finals, so they dance in front all night like they won. They'll bad mouth the judges, their partners, or say the event didn't mean anything in the first place. Another example: A teacher makes off-hand, dismissive or rude remarks about another teacher when that teacher is referenced or praised.

- **ENTITLEMENT:** The Nissy holds unreasonable expectations of special treatment and automatic compliance to them because they consider themselves special. Any failure to comply with their expectations is considered an attack on their perceived superiority, which often triggers what's called Narcissistic Rage. Example: A high level dancer doesn't make finals, rips off their number, stomps it on the floor and curses. Another example: A couple doesn't place how they thought they should have, and publicly yells at the event director, contest coordinator or competitor liaison.

- **MAGICAL THINKING:** Nissy's see themselves as perfect using distortion and illusion known as Magical Thinking. They will dump shame onto others who don't support their views. Example: Teachers who teach without real training. They may do well competitively and start teaching immediately.They are amazing at making up rules, sayings and teachings on the spot to protect their views, and will have no issue with referencing other respected instructors as "irrelevant, out of date, nonsensical," etc. etc. Another example: An Event Director will change history, facts and agreements in their heads to save money. They will attempt to shame an instructor, judge or volunteer into accepting lower wages or returns by questioning their value, their time given, etc, etc.

- **BAD BOUNDARIES:** The Nissy does not recognize that others are separate from themselves. Others exist to meet their needs or may as well not exist at all. Example: A leader who is off-time dances with a follower who is on-time. The leader wraps his thumb and/or whole hand into a grip around her hand or wrist to control her, despite the rough and dangerous position it puts her hand and arm in. Another example: A promoter finds a competitors flyers on the flyer table and either removes them and replaces them with their own, or simply places their own on top of the competitor's flyers.

- **ENVY:** A Nissy inflates their sense of superiority in the face of another person's skills or attention by using contempt against them. Example: A dancer takes his partner and dances in front, blocking a birthday girl having her birthday dance. Another example: A good dancer is in town. The Nissy, used to being the center of attention, asks the better dancer to dance but grimaces, looks bored or overpowers the better dancer in order to publicly diminish the better dancer.

- **EXPLOITATION:** Can take many forms, but always involves the exploitation of others without regard to their feelings or interest. They put the other in a subservient position where resistance would be difficult or even impossible. The subservience is not so much real as assumed. Example: A leader sees his follower as the subservient. Instead of the follower being danced, they are danced around. The leader expands while the follower contracts.

As I write about the sin of EXPLOITATION, I'm struck once again with the fact that the largest percentage of Nissies in our community are men. Women are catching up, but it started with the men.) And no wonder. To lead a woman in Abstract Improvisation is a Narcissists' dream. And I believe it's why talented women are leaving our sport in droves, but the ones replacing them are women who are wounded themselves... enablers... women and girls who base their identity on the approval of men, not an internal sense of power and worth. This has to be stopped.

Now that I've used a lot of big words, and have probably scared you a little, I've gone ahead and made it a little more simple. Here are some "less wordy" ways to pinpoint a Nissy in your dance community:

- **They Dance in Front:** No matter what level they are, they believe people want to see them dance more than better or more respected dancers. They will not give way to a champion dancer, and some will actually run into the champion dancer in order to make them obtain more room.

- **They Appear Supremely Confident:** They stand out on the social and competition floor with their fantastically stylish dress, cocky attitudes and triumphant glow. Judges constantly put them in because they APPEAR successful, despite horrific errors in lead, follow, timing and footwork. Drop your eyes to a dancer's feet and count with the music. You will be surprised how many make finals with a four (or three, or three and three quarters) count push break, if they are even on beat at all.

- **They Don't Take Lessons:** Nissies believe they can take one workshop and teach it the next day. They think they are an expert in the dance a month in. If they do take, it's with another Nissy, and they don't get any better, just more arrogant on the floor.

- **They Have Terrible Floor Craft:** They will not recognize another couple's established slot, even if part of the couple is an established dancer of a higher level. Again, the world exists to serve them, so your slot is their slot, should they need it.

- **They are Easily Disagreeable:** If you, as a partner, do not smile, help show them off, help them win or do exactly as they expect, they will become moody, pouty, impatient and even angry, no matter what their level. The higher the level, it seems, the more this happens, but it may depend on location.

- **They Point the Finger:** It is always someone else's fault. If they don't make finals, it's the judges, the music or their partner's fault. If they don't place, their partner didn't give it all they had or the judges were meanspirited, unfair and out to "get them."

- **Their Partner Isn't Seen:** If a Nissy is dancing with someone who ISN'T another Nissy, then the healthy person is overpowered, overshadowed and in general thrown around. If the partner ever tries to shine, the Nissy will not light up in delight at the creativity of their partner, but rather, will look annoyed, interrupted or impatient unless their partner's actions are helping them win.

You probably have a few in mind, but honestly, there are a lot more that just aren't easy to spot. You'll figure them out over time. After all, the more powerful in the community they are, the more they know the criteria I just listed is easy to spot.

The true NPD's that have been around for awhile are charming, witty and can talk their way out of everything. They sound amazing. They sound brilliant. They can clown and make you laugh. They make you feel so very special when you're around them. They make you want to fight for them. They make you feel like they were wronged if they don't get their way. But after being within close quarters of them for a while, during a private lesson, workshop or meeting... when you walk away, you have a small tiny fear of their disapproval, of getting on their bad side, or a need and a determination to stay on their good side. You don't glow with self improvement. You don't feel empowered. You are left wanting... wanting to be around them again, wanting to be like them and wanting to have their approval.

But here's the thing. As I said before:

"A narcissist is not capable of putting the organizations (i.e., studio's, club's, partner's, community's) needs before his or her own needs."

Remember that. And remember that their "needs" aren't normal or healthy needs, like the need for 'unquestioning' worship or praise, or the need to win, no matter how it's done or what the cost is to the event, their competitors and sometimes even their partners. A Nissy promoter "needs" their community to accept no one but the teachers and pros only they deem worthy. A Nissy DJ "needs" to be the only DJ in town and a Nissy club owner "needs" the other clubs to either shut down or not interfere with their nights and their "money," no matter how it limits the community, weakens it or divides it.

I have seen studios literally close because of Nissies. I have seen entire clubs shut down because of Nissies. I have have seen dancers injured and put out for more than a year because of Nissies. I have seen the words of a Nissy stay with a person for decades and eat away at them. The Nissies have wreaked havoc upon our communities across the planet. Why?

The Nissies have great power when it comes to the unsuspecting public. We don't expect underhanded tactics. We don't expect that the rules of common decency aren't held by everyone. We don't believe it when we hear they've tried to run others out of town, or placed their dances on top of the only successful night others go to. We who are healthy in swing tend to believe the best in people, and we don't see Nissies coming. Rules don't apply to Nissies. They truly, honestly and 100% believe they have the right to destroy anyone in anyway who stands between them and what they want.

Bottom line?

**Nissies don't build a community;
they create their own.**

I encourage you to watch for the Nissy or Nissies on your dance floor. Remember, they can only wreak havoc when then decend upon the "unsuspecting" public. But if you are on the lookout, you can avoid much of their devastation.

Watch for them. They are the people you feel driven to please. They are the people you feel like you never get a good dance with, no matter how hard you try, and you feel like it's all your fault... because they are *"just SO good!"* (sarcasm intended). They are the people who, quite often, seem "cool" or "in." And above all, know that **it will take bravery to identify them**.

Understand that Nissies do not take it well when you no longer hold them in admiration, and most of their followers or enablers will have learned well not to question them. Often your community will not want to support you in your first separation efforts. It's difficult to label anyone when everyone around you is in 'hero-worship' mode, but it can be done.

Once you start to suspect someone, especially someone who seems incredibly charming and well-loved, you may want to second guess yourself. Don't. Your gut is one of the greatest gifts we've all been given. And believe me, once you finally do admit that they are a Nissy, or in a Nissy-like stage, I promise you... it will save yourself a great deal of stress you didn't realize you had! Trust me. And you'll enjoy your dancing a whole lot more. Believe me.

And then, once you know who they are, I encourage you... do not feed into their frenzy. Don't bother dancing with them unless you must. You can say yes when they ask you, but most of the time they expect others to make the effort to dance with them. Don't bother chasing after them. It's just not worth it, on any level. Re-read their characteristics. Get to know the consequences that come with interacting with a Nissy. That's not what partner dancing is about.

I am aware that many Nissies feel the need to ask the better dancers in the room, just to prove they can out-dance them. I always turn these leaders down. I can see them coming a mile away, and it's just not worth my physical health to put my technical abilities in the blender of their subpar novice thrashings or their narcissistic rage. But a Nissy is the only kind of dancer I will turn down. I'll dance with anyone of any level, novice and newcomer included, who treats me with respect.

We all deserve respect on the dance floor. It's a non-negotiable in partner dancing. No matter who you are or what level of experience you have, your physical, mental and emotional well being should be respected on the dance floor. And when that's missing from one of the partners, damage almost always follows. From feeling discarded, ugly or demeaned to sprained wrists, backs and shoulders, the dangers and risks are more than you can imagine. Until it happens to you. So try not to persue their attention if you can. It'll save you a "woulda, coulda, shoulda" story of your own.

On the plus side of things, Nissies are usually attracted to one another. They travel in little groups or packs, and gather in the same clubs and locations. As such, I recommend you find a monthly or a weekly dance where they don't feel special and then enjoy dancing with normal, healthy and more satisfying dancers. Try the same method with conventions too- most are riddled with Nissies nowadays, but there are still certain events where Nissies just wouldn't be "showcased." So it helps to look for the places Nissies are avoiding, and enjoy yourself. Who in the world wants to dance with a partner who is absolutely NOT interested in you, protecting your needs, your physical well being on the dance floor? Dancing's better when the person wants to dance *with* you, not *at* you.

I'm serious. Let me emphasis this again.

Partner dancing is, at its very core, an agreement between two people to love, respect and honor one another on the dance floor in order to create and enjoy a beautiful, intimate, exciting and fun experience that dancing on our own cannot create.

The Nissy will never know the potential gifts of partner dancing beyond that of being "seen" and gaining power. When two Nissies draw each other, they are in total bliss. Both want extreme exposure and both go for it… whether it mean knocking others out of their way, rolling on the floor or sticking out their tongues to get it. But that's the kind of bliss only two Nissies would ever take pleasure in. And it's not what partner dancing is all about.

If you want your partner to *see* you and dance *with* you, just say NO to the Nissy.

Bravely,
Katherine Eastvold

Saturday, April 9th 2011

Routines 101

What Makes a Great Routine...GREAT

Dancing can reveal all the mystery that music conceals.
- Charles Baudelaire

I rarely enjoy anything as much as I enjoy choreographing. Besides the people, it is the thing I miss most about my owning my own studio. It was life changing, empowering and incredibly satisfying to choreograph all day long... Foxtrot, Cha Cha, Waltz, West Coast Swing and Salsa... everything!

Then love, marriage and life happened. Now that I'm traveling for the WCS community again, it's been a little shocking. I'm discovering that many widely known benefits and expectations of putting a routine together have been lost over the years. Things that used to be universally known or expected are now, I'm discovering, completely lost and forgotten. I've found this to be true for much of our dance, not just the area of routines and choreography, but I shall address that in the future.

But if you or someone you know is interested in doing a West Coast Swing routine, and you want to get the most out of it that you can, here are some things you should know before you even pick a partner, nevermind a song or a choreographer.

THE UNIVERSAL GOAL

Whether you're starting on this journey to get better, to make your partner happy, to showcase your accomplishments or to make your coach happy, at the heart of it all you really have only one goal that matters: to put YOUR best foot forward. The audience will only see YOU. And nobody else can be you. Nobody! And that's a GREAT thing!

West Coast Swing is stunning in its ability to showcase your individuality within its strict parameters. So the main goal of your routine should be to showcase *your* strengths, *your* stylings, *your* lines, *your* footwork and *your own* personality.

I have choreographed routines for students with movements that look terrible on me. Don't roll your eyes. I have enough students do that. I'm serious- there are moves that I would never ever, in a million years, allow myself to be videotaped doing, nevermind putting into a routine of mine to be played repeatedly by others. However, those moves have often worked for others beautifully. If they look fantastic on my student, I'm putting it in.

Take my husband Nick versus my dance partner Josh. Both Nick and I have long forearms, but very short upper arms. When we do routines together, such as our Salsa routine, there are drops, tricks and moves that work, and then quite a few that don't. However, Josh has super long slim arms. They eliminate certain moves Nick and I do, but they also open up quite a few moves Nick and I cannot do without my head getting caught in his armpit or my hair tangled in his wrist. Naturally a lot of this is learned the hard way, but it's an expected part of the routine process.

In short, choreography is sometimes about your dance level, but quite often it's about other things you can't change. When Josh and I first partnered up, we'd never really danced together. So I videotaped us dancing to a few songs, and very quickly noticed that our legs were the exact same length. If you know my routines, you'll notice that I very much capitalized on that in my choreography. But I also noticed that our arms were completely and utterly different. Therefore I had to eliminate all "in-sync" arm stylings. If Josh's arm was up in a long line, my arm would stay down in its own line, not parallel to his, as you see here.

Choreography that capitalized on our strengths and smoothed over our differences: arms vs. legs, etc.

Any choreographer should know about these expected similarities and differences, and be able to see it. Even if they can't explain why as I just did, they should understand certain moves and stylings don't work on every single couple they give choreography to.

Yes, long distance choreography is popular today. You send

music to a choreographer and they send you a video with your choreography back. If that's the case, then you need to choose your choreographer very wisely, or be prepared to change your choreography accordingly, either on your own or with another coach or choreographer.

Because of the Universal Goal, I've also choreographed routines to music that doesn't move me, but it moves my students. It's not difficult to do, unless the music doesn't match the kind of dance they want choreographed. For example, a wedding couple brings in "At Last" as their wedding song, and they want a Cha Cha routine.

Okay, that's an extreme example, but still, people today rarely know what kind of music works with what kind of dance (thank you very much, *Dancing with the Stars* and "iPod" DJ's!). I've been lucky to work with couples who have had, for the most part, swingable songs. And though they don't match my tastes, I can tell how much a couple loves their song. And so I wrap the choreography around their passion for it so that the audience can see *their* hearts on the floor.

I remember one couple that had already won the US Open in their division. They were trying a completely new direction and had received choreography for a 100% lyrical song. But they loved it. I mean, they really really loved this song. Even though it was chosen for them by somebody else, I could see that it made them want to feel. But they held back. And since the song wasn't swing, it made the choreography they'd been given seem akward.

Yes, I fixed a lot of the choreography, but my biggest change was to how they approached the song while dancing. I said, "Look, you love this song. I can see it. Don't hide it! Let it envelop and fill you all the way through and just groove to it while you dance it. I want you to get totally lost in the song." And so they did. And it gave me goosebumps.

Later, when they did their next "demo" in preparation for the Open, my own coach came up to me and said they had tears in their eyes after watching them. She said, "I didn't know they could dance like that." Exactly. It wasn't a swing song, and it was hardly a swing dance, but all of that and the akwardness it would normally have produced made the performance one of their best yet. As a judge, my job would have been easy, but as an audience member, I would have thouroughly enjoyed seeing "them," in all their joy and passion, enjoy their song the way only they could.

(Imagine if they did that with a real swing song and a real swing routine! Oh my. I believe it would've brought the house down! And they would've placed much higher. There is nothing on this planet like watching swing dancers jam out their alive-ness in full expansion, with unfettered feet, against a ridiculously awesome swing song. It's better than a triple shot of espresso, and it'll charge you with so much energy you won't be able to sleep that night! But I digress...)

The fact remains that no matter who you are, no matter what your background, level or experience, it's vital that you understand this one thing before anything else.

If you are going to invest the money, the time, the training and the practicing... make sure you keep one goal in mind: **to be yourselves.** <u>Never</u> underestimate an audience. They know if you are pretending to be somebody else. And <u>never</u> underestimate the power of your "true self." It will fight you every step of the way if you try to be something you're not. You'll reduce your hours of investment, practice and coaching while increasing your enjoyment and benefits of the routine by taking the steps to ensure that it reflects YOU… and no one else.

YOUR MUSIC

This may sound obvious, but at the core you are doing a DANCE routine. Whether or not you're competing or simply showcasing your routine, never forget that you're doing a *dance* routine. So pick a song that makes you want to do just that: DANCE. And no, head-bobbing doesn't count. It has to make you want to get *off* the couch, not lay back on it.

Trust me, whatever song or combination of songs you pick, you will end up hearing it a million-ba-jillion times before you ever perform it. You'll hear it at slow speeds, at fast speeds, in your head while you take a shower and in your head while trying to go to bed. If it inspires you to *dance*, and dance *now*, you'll enjoy the entire routine process and every performance a lot more than if not.

I am not a morning person. Not even a little bit. I don't now how in the world I survived teaching high school and I don't now how in the world I'll ever survive kids. When the sun rises, I get tired and when it falls, I start to rev up. So when I have to stumble out of bed for a 6 AM floor trial with only three hours of sleep, I've never had to worry about not having the energy to practice. I put in the time and the work to get the right song. I know that, without a doubt, I'm going to want to dance no matter what the moment the DJ hits play.

The same applies to you. If you're a morning person, then you're going to have to be ready to dance at 11 PM at night. Either way, have a song that starts your engine is everything. Help yourself out and take the time to pick the right song ahead of time. It's worth the investment.

While we're on the subject of music, let me let you in on a little secret. We pros with real training know that you choreograph, practice and rehearse to music that is 2% slower than what you will actually perform to on stage. You see, we know that adrenaline will make the speed you're used to feel like mud when you're out there.

Some pros no longer do this in WCS because they are no longer nervous. They know exactly how they are going to place or there is very little at stake. Others no longer do this because they are no longer energized by their routines or the crowd. But the majority of the real professionals dance it at 1 or 2% up from what they practice to, and for everyone else, 2% is considered the hard and fast rule. And what a little nugget of gold that rule is. I can't even tell you. It's quite the performance booster.

So if your song is 130 bpm, you may want to practice and choreograph at 2% down and then make a CD with your song at its normal speed. Or, as most people do, practice and rehearse at its normal speed, and then ask the DJ at the event to increase it by 2% when they play it. NOT at floor trials, mind you, but only for the big show. Trust me, you won't notice a difference out there at all! The adrenaline will make it feel as if it's the normal speed you've been practicing to all along, which will give your performance a much greater shot at being smooth and powerful.

YOUR PARTNER

I'm not going to lie. Partnerships are not easy. They are like marriages. They take mutual work, conviction, love, honor, respect and humor to run smoothly. I think I've seen a perfectly equal partnership on all fronts... twice. I learned very early on that for every two minutes we see of a partnership on the convention floor, there are hundreds to sometimes thousands of hours that we aren't seeing of that partnership. But it's those hours that really matter, much more than those 2.5 minutes on the floor.

So here's the deal: everyone's different. Some people need a 50/50 partnership. Some can handle 90/10 partnerships. Decide what you can handle and grab a partner that fits. Be aware that most partnerships break up before they ever make it to the floor. There's no shame in that at all. Have pride for trying because you will have learned a lot no matter how far into the process you made it. It's worth the risk.

Keep this in mind, too. No matter how many times you've heard it, height, hair color and body types are NOT the thing to look for in a partner. All of that can be solved in choreography and costuming. Michelle Kinkaid was more than a full head taller than Phil Trau when they won the US Open Classic Division three times in a row. They rocked it like nobody's business out there. Lance Shermoen, the King of the US Open, danced with more than three different partners over two decades, none of whom looked anything alike, and all of whom were phenomenal dancers. Yes, all of the routines looked different, just as they should have, but they were all amazing. Looks and levels don't matter. Those can be worked around in routines.

What does matter? **Abuse.** You absolutely must be on the lookout for that. Routines are highly stressful projects. The tend to bring out the absolute worst in the absolute best of us. No one is immune. Verbal abuse, emotional abuse and mental abuse... these are the greatest pitfalls of routines. Learn how recognize the signs, how to protect yourself and when to walk away. If you have a partner that respects and honors you, no matter what their level, you can get an incredibly satisfying and even highly successful routine experience.

YOUR CHOREOGRAPHY

Oh there are so many things to know about choreography! Especially in today's environment. It is only too easy to pay a ton of money and get a routine you can't dance all the way through after even as much as a month of practicing. Now, more than ever, you must be attentive, aware and ready when it comes to choreography.

Here are things things to know:

A) If you plan on hiring a choreographer, remember that you don't have to pick only one.

Some couples have two, three or even four choreographers work on their routine. But whoever you work with, be aware that it's easy to be intimidated and accept changes, choreography or music out of fear (submission) rather than trust (joy). I don't think people understand how much fear controls their decisions in today's climate.

One of my most life-changing lessons was that a business attracts people who are like the person who owns it. We've had Nissies running and winning things for more than decade now, and so we've spent the last decade slowly but surely losing teachers who are healthy and helpful and replacing them with Nissy instructors, who are more interested in their own visions and desires than they are in you and your success.

As a result, it will be quite easy, no matter where you live, to end up getting choreography from a Nissy. And you will instinctively fear them enough to stay quiet. Very quiet. Watch what your body does when you are around them. It will tell you wonders. Last year, for example, I was working on a couple's routine for the US Open. They were taking with another coach at the same time. At floor trials, as I worked with them, they were open, giddy and asking a lot of questions. They had freedom.

Then it was time for me to work with another couple. I went up into the bleachers. As I waited for the couple to take the floor, I noticed that the "other" coach had approached the couple I was just working with. My jaw dropped. The woman's shoulders were wrapped tight around her body. Both of them were kind of hunched over. The coach was chattering away super fast as I've seen him do before, even with me. But I'm strong enough that I'm not afraid of him, and I can chatter away right back rather easily. But the couple never said a word. Literally. I think she kind of nodded her head at one point, but for the most part, they were caught in his Nissy tractor beam. They looked deflated by the meeting, the exact opposite effect you want from a coach. But he was a 'name,' and he had youthful energy, so still and quiet they stayed. In fear.

How unfortunate. And how easily avoidable! So take note. Fear will slow you down, cost you more and paralyze you. A good coach and choreographer will make you feel empowered and excited about getting on the floor. Remember, this is your routine. It's your time and it's your money and it's your performance. Only. Nobody else's.

As the old saying goes, "the only one who can fight for you is... YOU." If you fight to choose your choreographer wisely before you begin, as in doing some research, taking some privates to see how they operate or asking around... you'll save yourself the pain of breaking up with the choreographer in the middle of the routine. You might have change mid-choreography, but be assured that this happens so incredibly often these days, that I've never heard of a single pro asking where their couple has gone once they've lost them. Very few are keeping track the way they used to, and if they are, then that's kind of a red flag anyway. So enjoy flexing your freedom muscles.

B) Don't be afraid to ask!

9 out of 10 couples I've seen in the last four years have had their choreography done by one pro and then partially or completely re-choreographed by another pro in order to "fix" it. This isn't cheap. But this expensive practice is perpetuated by a nonsensical trend: couples give their original choreographer credit and label the other choreographers as "coaches." I constantly see couples hit with surprise at the routine they've received, simply because the choreography that inspired them in others was actually done by a completely different pro. So when you ask a couple where they got their routine, find out exactly what pro choreographed your favorite parts. It'll save you a lot of money in the long run. Then pay it forward. Give credit where credit is due.

C) And finally, don't be afraid to make your own changes.

You can keep yourself in check by videotaping yourself. You'll learn what to keep and what to toss and, depending on your eye, save yourself a lot of money in coaching and choreography. If something feels awkward, stop watching the video for the eighth time and change it to feel less awkward. Sometimes it's something as simple as turning your shoulders or hips to a different wall that makes everything feel better. Sometimes it's putting in more footwork to protect your knee from being twisted. Trust your body to tell you when something isn't working right, and do what needs to be done to fix it. You don't even need to point out the change to your coach.

Too often I see couples making a change they love, and then they show their coach, like proud teenagers wanting their mom's approval. But the coach feels threatened instead, and makes another change to it. Now the couple is uncomfortable again, and avoid making any changes in the future out of "consideration" for their coach. If you have a feeling it'll go that way, then just enjoy your changes on your own... and you'll rock it a lot harder on that floor as a result.

THE MAGIC BEAN: PHRASING

When I was studying at UCLA I was hired as one of their fitness instructors. During training, they pounded one big lesson into our heads again and again: choreograph to the **major phrase**. I had already learned about phrasing in Swing, but was surprised to find it so underlined in a fitness program. The staff would literally fire instructors who didn't phrase their fitness choreography. Why? Because whether you're educated in music or not, your body knows a major phrase change when it hears one.

The UCLA trainers considered our training in phrasing as a "protective measure" against injuries. If we choreographed our step routines, for example, to start over on the major phrase, the body's internal instinct to change is fed, and nobody trips or falls over by instinctively changing when the music does but the choreography doesn't. I've seen a few of those falls go down. It's not pretty.

UCLA knew phrasing was a powerful tool, and back then, swing did too. Being able to 'chart' a song is everything.

It's a powerful and easy tool that will make your routine look amazing, more professional and more exciting to your friends, family and audiences. So whether you are choreographing your own routine or bringing it to someone else, try to phrase out your music or hire someone else to phrase it out before even touching it with choreography. Make sure you start a new pattern on the "1" of each major phrase.

So there you are. Doing a routine is **not** a small task. I didn't even touch on costumes! Or Timing, Technique or Teamwork (any coach that has any actual training will build these into you and the choreography they give your to make you both look and feel fabulous!). But it's worth it. And worthwhile things take work.

I'm keenly aware that one routine can impact every level of dancer in the audience, no matter what division or what place the judges give you. I'm not a fan of routines that are clearly unrehearsed, uncomfortable or uncontrolled... the things that make your eyes gloss over while watching them. C.S. Lewis once said, "No book is really worth reading at the age of ten which is not equally - and often far more - worth reading at the age of fifty and beyond." I believe it's the same with choreography. If a routine I put on the floor doesn't make kids and kings want to dance, then I've wasted my time.

As the nature of Jack & Jill's change, as more and more people are injured, and as more and more people feel sidelined in the dance, routines have the potential to change things. For the good or the bad. Follow these tips though, and you'll be part of changing things for the better. You can love, live and grow through routines... visibly expand and shine... if you take the right steps.

Above all, I wish you the strength and courage to be yourselves out there...

and NO ONE ELSE!

Thursday, April 21st 2011

Just Say It
You Know More Than You Think You Do

The majority of the real talent in our dance community is in crisis. Professionals, champions, judges and advanced dancers of today and of the past *(when the All-Star Division didn't exist)* are doubting themselves. Though they have extensive knowledge, training, insight, control, centering, impeccable timing, posture, technique and individual footwork and stylings, they are, by and large, questioning themselves. Some are retiring, some are switching to other dances and some are quitting dancing altogether. It's nothing short of tragic.

You have the power to stop it. I'm going to tell you how.

I noticed something at the national dance events across the nation this last year. An irritating yet thankfully inconsistent failure in our judging system of the past is now a full-blown and snarling monster in the present. It happened at every single event. The results would be announced: fifth place *(murmurs)*, fourth place *(more murmurs)*, third place *(fidgety panic),* second

place (*impending gloom and hope at the same time*) and then...
First.

BOOM! The whispers, even cries all around me erupt. "What happened to so & so?" "What did I miss?" "That's insane." "Maybe it's because they danced early?" "Maybe the scores were wrong?" and the worst, "That's just wrong."

I've been dancing WCS for nearly 20 years now. I've been to competitions since my start. I've been at almost every awards presentation. And if you know me, you know I have a killer memory. I remember them like it was yesterday. So I *know* when the sand is shifting. Okay, not shifting... more like quaking. A huge fissure has erupted. And the land of "performance" now looks over a huge canyon to the distant ledge of "scores."

This is not the typical, "oh, I had fourth and fifth switched," or "I had first place in third," or "I didn't have them in there at all" that I used to hear at so many events long, long ago. In fact, I was known for literally calling every single one of the scores back then. Even when I was a newcomer. I didn't know names and I didn't know faces, but I knew performance. And every once in a while, I'd wonder how my 3rd place was switched with my 5th place, but I never, and I mean NEVER saw a routine that I was sure would place... not place. None of us did.

Once the Points system was introduced though, around 1996, things definitely changed in that arena. Pros wanted to politic and protect their money and started fudging the scores a little. But in general, talented dancers won over untrained dancers. Messy, cocky 'know-it-all's' who didn't bother training but relied on "flash and trash" were kept in the lower ranks until they were serious and started showing some effort, skill and training.

But not today. Today is different. Very, very different.

Today there is a complete and utter disconnect between the famed "Three T's" (Timing, Technique and Teamwork) and the final results. Audiences watch as a dance that was clearly executed with incredible craftsmanship, timing, teamwork and technique, as well as incredibly inspiring swing content, play and footwork, with no missed leads, no quivers in balance... just pure, inspiring, get-you-on-your-feet dancing... is left completely in the cold. As in out of the top five altogether. No recognition. Nothing. Some aren't even close. And some, perhaps most tragically of all, are, for no reason I can imagine, at the bottom.

This, of course, has not gone unnoticed. At all. Even by the winners.

I'm watching the *true* professionals walk to the podium with a look pure confusion. They know their dance was a train wreck. A *true* craftsman knows when they were awarded for something unworthy of praise. They look uncomfortable... a bit wary. (Not the Nissy, of course. They always deserve, and completely expect, a walk to the podium, or even a higher placement, yes?)

The audiences? The ones that used to hear the scores and break into discussions like, "I had them here, but I guess I could see them there. What about you?" That audience is not taking it quietly. They, for the first time since I've been around, are flooding the scoring rooms. They didn't even compete, but they want to know what the heck happened to produce such out of touch results.

I repeat. Non-competitors are checking the scores. I've never seen anything like it. In droves. They are baffled, concerned, unclear or just in awe and they are looking for answers. Every Sunday night, as I sit and listen to them, I hear their conclusions. I am only going to list the conclusions I have heard from at least three different dancers each:

- *The judges put in the people who are on their own event's staff.*
- *The judges put in whoever danced the closest to the way they did when they competed.*
- *The judges were all over the board.*
- *The judges were scared of not being hired again.*
- *The judges put in who the event directors asked them too.*
- *The judges put in who they thought would win, not should win.*

Let me be clear. The point of this article is not the judging that's happening today. That's an entirely separate article, though I do think a few of these reasons are spot on.

Now, my point is that, when you love what a couple does out there... you are not the only one! When the scores don't make sense to you, chances are, there's a sea of people standing right next to you that feels the same way you do.

You know more than you think you do.

But I'm asking you to do more than trust yourself. I am asking you take a deep breath, take a chance, and tell the talented person you saw that they inspired you. You can do it by email, by social network or in person. It can be brief: "I loved your Jack & Jill!" Or it can be detailed: "I loved that section with the (fill in the blank)." Of course, there's my personal favorite "You were robbed. That was the best dancing on the floor hands down." You'll always hear me say, "give credit where credit is due." When the judges don't follow through on this concept, I'm telling you right now: **you can.**

This applies to social dancing as well. If you see a dancer on the floor who is a true champion, in skill, talent and control... a true artist that you just want to stare at because you learn so much by watching them, because they make you want to dance till your feel fall off... tell them. No matter who they are.

There is power in this approach. It WILL make a difference. Early on in my dance career a number of people said they loved my anchor. Let me tell you, I've never stopped paying attention to my anchor since then. If you tell someone you love their footwork or their lead or their smile while they dance, you can bet they are going to remember that and keep it in their dancing.

As such, I've made it a habit since I was very young to compliment those dancers that gave me goose bumps, no matter who they were or what it was that they danced. I knew even then that if I wanted to see more of such inspiration, then direct praise was in order. Now it's your turn.

It's time to inspire our truly talented dancers to stay with WCS. The days are far gone when a highly trained, talented and skilled dancer didn't need anyone telling them that to know it. In an era where timing and technique are no longer rewarded but attitude, falling and Nissy-ish-ness are, the talented dancers are questioning their talent. They are questioning their place in this world.

**In the dark and quiet,
they are wondering if the world has gone mad.**

Please... give them the credit that they are due. Please... you know more than you think you do. Please...

Just Say It.

Thursday, April 28th 2011

West Coast Swing Essentials
How to Recognize West Coast Swing

I learned a massive amount while owning a studio. About life, about dance, about everything. But one of the favorite things I learned was that there is a dance for every season of life. I opened the studio a committed West Coast Swing fan, and left the studio a fully obsessed fan of *all* the partner dances... from Viennese Waltz to Tango, to Bolero.

A dance studio draws you closer to people unlike any other kind of business. It's a family. You get to see people at their best, at their worst and everything in between. And you get to see that there is a need for all of the dances. For the street dances, the latin dances and the smooth dances. There's even a need for American and International styles. Every dance matches a person, a people and a family. And in life we all experience different seasons that draw us or push us closer to the different dances that can heal or feed us at the time.

As time went on, through a thousand privates, classes and

workshops with questioning and exploring students of all levels and backgrounds, I had the amazing opportunity to learn the intimate details that make a Waltz a Waltz, a Salsa a Salsa and a Cha Cha a Cha Cha. I learned that every partner dance has a character, a step pattern, a pulse and a particular floor craft. West Coast Swing is no different.

It too is a partner dance that's lead-and-follow and danced on beat, with steps, rhythms, rules and a specific floor craft. In fact, its rules are quite a bit more complex than any other dances.' So what are the essential elements that help us identify the dance? How do we know when we're watching a WCS dance and not a Tango, a Foxtrot... or even Abstract Improvisation or Zouk?

To help, here are some easy things to look for when you're trying to identify a couple's WCS content:

THE WEST COAST SWING ESSENTIALS

#1
A DEFINED RECTANGLE SLOT

Country Two Step travels around the floor, as does Waltz. Salsa is danced in more of a small circle, as is East Coast Swing. West Coast Swing, however, is danced in what's called a "slot." Most teachers teach that your slot should run parallel to the wood panels of the floor you are dancing on. Others say it should be danced parallel to the longest side of a rectangle room. I say that no matter where you are, make sure your slot isn't in the opposite direction of anyone else's around you. That kind of behavior never ends well.

A WCS slot is typically 2-3 floor squares (6 to 8 ft) long and one floor square wide. Most WCS dancers that have been dancing it for the last 30 to 60 years, however, typically stay in the 6 feet or less range when it comes to length. They focus heavily on the footwork and tend to dance, even now, on extremely crowded floors, so their slot has remained tight and controlled.

The Slot and its Boundaries

In WCS, depending upon the available room, we can shift the Defined Slot's location on the floor, but then we re-post and stay there in a new established slot or return back to our original slot. WCS is NOT a rounded or unconfined dance. The slot does <u>not</u> extend very far on any one side.

#2
MAN IN THE MIDDLE

In WCS, from the point of an onlooker, the man is visually in the center and patterns are used to move the woman up and down the slot. The man and woman do not stay at opposite ends of the slot and then switch, and the woman *does not* stay in the center while he moves around her unless it's to let her pass him on her way down the slot. He stays in the middle, and makes magic moving her up, down, in and out of the slot. Some call the man's actions to pin down the center of the slot 'posting.'

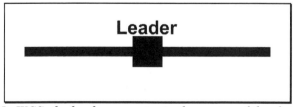

In WCS, the leader operates in the center of the slot.

Here are other ways "Man in the Middle" plays out in the WCS slot:

At the start of a WCS dance, the follower begins in closed position with the man in the center of the slot:

For the majority of a WCS dance, the follower begins and ends all patterns at one of the ends of the slot:

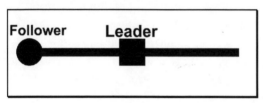

In the Push Break, the follower moves towards the leader, then returns to her previous position. The whip follows a similar pattern:

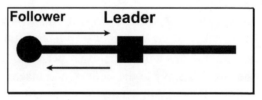

In side passes, such as the Underarm Turn, the Left Side Pass or the Tuck, etc., the follower moves from one end of the slot to the other. Notice how the leader, throughout all the patterns, remains in the center of the slot:

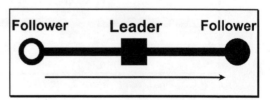

Graphics by Katherine Eastvold

3
SENTENCE STRUCTURE

WCS patterns are a lot like a sentence. They have a beginning, a middle and an end. The beginning of a WCS pattern is started by what's called a Rubber Band motion. It occurs on the '& a 1' of a pattern and provides the momentum for the follower to move towards the leader. The middle of the sentence starts with the double-triple I will talk about in essential #4. The middle can come in the form of a myriad of patterns. Because WCS has so many triples and so many basics, the variety of patterns available are remarkable. They always require a multitude of triples, however, mixed in with a few doubles and every once in a while, a single, depending on the music that's playing.

No matter how long a WCS pattern ends up being, no matter how long the sentence goes on, it will always end with a period. In the case of WCS, we call this an anchor. For years teachers have taught that the anchor is the period at the end of a sentence, but it does require some unique training and as such, much of its power and technique has been lost.

The anchor always takes place while the man is in the center and the woman is at the end of a slot. The anchor is primarily a function of the center (your center point of balance, also called your solar plexus by some). However, the motion of your center during an anchor is incredibly small. It will be easier for most to simply watch the feet and see if they gather together at the end of a pattern and seem to re-ground themselves.

An anchor, unless the song ends, is followed by the '& a 1' rubber band motion, the beginning of the next sentence… the beginning of the next pattern. Sometimes you will see a couple "extend" a pattern at the end of the slot. It looks like the couple is about to start a new sentence, but instead, they do some playful footwork in place. This conversational kind of dancing is still part of the previous sentence.

But when the play has come to an end, you will see the couple start a new pattern with a very clear WCS '& a 1' rubber band that gets them in motion once again and the new sentence or pattern takes off.

#4
DOUBLE, TRIPLE START

This is probably one of the easiest characteristics to identify. It's quite the powerful tool. In short, all West Coast Swing patterns, whether they are basics or not, will begin with a double rhythm followed by a triple rhythm. For those that don't know what rhythms are, you can think of it this way: every pattern begins with a walk, walk followed by a triple step (or as one famous yet scattered teacher likes to say, "walk, walk, run-run-run!")

It is also important to recognize exactly how these two rhythms occur. At the start of a West Coast Swing pattern, look at the follower's feet. She will always start a pattern with her right foot and she will always travel towards the leader from the end of her slot. A double rhythm done in place does not qualify as the start of a WCS pattern.

The triple rhythm that follows is just as important. Other dances start with double rhythms too, but then they are followed by single or double rhythm, not by a triple rhythm. In WCS, that first double is always followed by a triple. What occurs on that triple varies greatly, depending on what basic or pattern is being done, but it will never be a single or a double rhythm. It will always be a triple. And it will always be in the center of the slot, when the partners are close to each other and the 'post.' At a more advanced level, this triple rhythm can even become a higher rhythm, depending on the pattern, like a quad, but you will never see it become less, like a double.

Do not be fooled by stutters. After years of telling dancers to remove their triples from their dancing in order to make way for this "new" dance, some are trying to bring them back in order to satisfy the judges. Unfortunately, it's not working. The majority of these dancers "stutter" instead of doing an actual triple step. A real triple step in WCS transfers the weight on '3   a4.' But stutters are different.

In stutters the so called "weight change" occurs on 'a3   4.' Not only are the beats incorrect, but these leaders never really transfer their weight. Typically, you will watch them simply tap their toe on the 'a' so that their 'a3' looks more like a hiccup, rather than an actual step or weight change. Often this tap occurs with no weight change at all, making their feet look busy when they really aren't.

When you are watching real WCS, you will see the triple rhythm executed on and between the 3 and the 4. Anything else is cheating and in bad form.

#5
AN ABUNDANCE OF TRIPLES

If you count out all the basic WCS patterns, you will notice that for almost every double rhythm, there are TWO triple rhythms. Not only that, but there are no single rhythms at all. Triple rhythms are much harder to do than single or double rhythms in a lead and follow dance, because they can't be danced 'split weight,' especially with good timing. Since the majority of other partner dances are made of single and double rhythms, WCS really stands out with its exciting triple rhythm footwork.

Once a dancer has mastered the above characteristics, meaning they are able to do them with all Three T's: Timing, Technique and Teamwork, then, and only then, does WCS provide the complex freedom for three unique characteristics. I call them the Higher Essentials.

Many try to skip past the mastery of the above skills and boundaries only to find themselves doing another dance entirely. But when the following characteristics are added to the core essentials of WCS, the results are truly incredible. The dance becomes addicting to all ages and generations. As with most art forms, once WCS is done with unusually excellent technique and skill, it can take anyone's breath away, dancer and non-dancer alike.

The following are the characteristics that again, are not required, but can be attained in WCS more than any other dance.

THE HIGHER ESSENTIALS

CONTRAST

Contrast is typically considered present when a WCS dance contains both small and subtle movements as well as large and fast ones. A dance that has nothing but big sweeping movements, dips and drops is considered to be only "one note."

Contrast is not simply speeding up and slowing down or reaching high then dropping low. Contrast is a higher essential, and as such requires an incredibly high level of dance skill, training and mastery. Contrast requires deft subtly combined with precise expansion. It's using an unexpected variety of movements to tell a story. Contrast draws people in… it prevents them from looking away… it keeps their attention and makes them hit the rewind button.

MUSICALITY

Musicality as a higher element goes beyond staying on beat. It means dancing to the major phrase (starting a new pattern on the 1 of major phrase in a song), doing a large movement to a large piece of music and a small movement to a small 'ting.' It's helping others hear things in the song they didn't know were even there. It's using the dance to paint a visual representation of the music. The more challenging the music, the more exciting the painting.

INDIVIDUAL STYLE

True WCS requires a high level of leading and following because it has eight basic patterns to build moves off of instead of one. Skilled WCS followers often have a very easy time switching into other partner dances because they've learned to follow anything. They can join any other class and immediately be able to follow the instructor, provided that the instructor is a good leader.

Along with the achievement of exquisite leading and following skill, WCS offers up the ability for both partners to add styling, footwork variations (syncopations), breaks and conversations through movement... all while staying in direct and perfect connection with their partner. The lead-follow relationship is never broken.

As such, each WCS dancer of this level looks unique. I chose to study WCS instead of ballroom at an early age because the ballroom ladies looked very "cookie-cutter." Real WCS allows one's individuality to appear within its strict confines. The more a dancer grows in the dance, the more individual their style becomes. If you're watching a floor where all the upper level women and men look the same, it's a clear indication that swing content is lacking.

It may be a challenge in the beginning to get used to catching each of these things, but your eye will soon learn and after a while, it will come naturally to you. Always start by watching the feet and listen closely to the beat of the music. This method works in identifying any partner dance, but since WCS is such a complex and difficult dance, easy shortcuts like this will get your further in less amount of time. So enjoy using these characteristics to identify WCS on your social floors, during competitions and during routines. But no matter what, as always...

KEEP ON DANCING!

Monday, May 23rd 2011

The Time Has Come

The Big One.

I've listened to our heartbeat.

For years now I've listened. I listened to former champions. I listened to fellow champions. I listened to newcomers. I listened to non-competitors. I listened to novice, intermediate, advanced and all-star dancers. I listened to judges, to event directors and to studio owners. I listened to DJ's. I listened to photographers. I even listened to hotel staff and to non-dancers staying in the hotels at conventions. I listened, and listened, and listened. I listened to the audiences and I listened to my students and I listened to the conversations taking place in hallways and dinner buffets and clubs. I listened. And I heard a lot. I heard what was being told, what was being said, what was being danced, what was being judged, what was being seen and what was being thought. I watched too. I watched carefully. I watched the Jack and Jill's, the social floor, the dancing during the breaks and the dancing during late night. I watched the routines, the workshops and the private lessons. I listened and heard and watched.

And by doing so, I ended up taking the pulse of our West Coast Swing community.

It's not good news. I learned that we are hurting. I learned that we are divided. I learned that we are in crisis. We are confused, damaged and torn. We are sad, angry and lost. I learned that we desperately need to see a doctor. It's time for a diagnosis. We need a prescription. We need to start healing and return to a state of joy, freedom and empowerment on the dance floor.

I can help. After absorbing, analyzing and assimilating all I had heard, seen and felt on the floor, I discovered The Big Picture. I know what's going on. And perhaps more importantly, I know how we got here.

Once I figured it out, I naturally started sharing it with others, as I usually do… in lessons, in discussions, in the hallways of conventions, etc. But this time it was different. People were gathering around to listen in. Many I knew, but many I didn't. Dancers passing by would hear my comments and would stop. They'd pull up a chair. They'd lean in. And I could see that they wanted more, much more.

At the US Open I gathered my biggest crowd yet. I believe it was Sunday afternoon, and by the time it had grown to cover and block two aisles, I realized it had become nothing more than a Q&A session… and I was able to easily answer ever Q with a very sound and thoroughly explained A. When it finally broke up for awards, I turned to my husband Nick and said, "I think I'd better start teaching on this stuff." He agreed.

So I spent December creating my SwingIN!s. A series of new and never-before-seen seminars, demonstrations and activities, I designed my SwingIN!s to give dancers what they so clearly desired: equipment for dancing in today's WCS world. I had no idea just how popular they would become.

My first one was held in January of this year (*Past, Present & Future*), where I first taught about how we got here. During it, I outlined and explained what I'd discovered about our history: The Gathering of Great Minds, The Renaissance and The Perfect Storm. The response was tremendous. The "ah ha!" moments were overwhelming. I could tell I had started something big.

As news of *Past, Present & Future* spread, so did the requests for encore seminars. I held numerous sold-out encore presentations of it in studios, living rooms and dance floors across southern California. At each, I reminded everyone that *Past, Present & Future* was designed to prepare them for "the big" SwingIN! that was coming in April on Easter weekend. I had named it *New School vs. Old School*, but it was really about much much more. For five hours on that Saturday afternoon, I taught, for the very first time, about my biggest discovery: Abstract Improvisation. It was nothing short of groundbreaking. Revolutionary.

And the attendees knew it.

When it was finally over, the dancers in attendance, that included newcomers, judges, promoters, instructors, competitors and social dancers... stood up, eyes opened, and... *danced their pants off that night!*

Then they spread the word.

It's been only a week and my terminology is appearing all over the social networks and my inbox is starting to fill. Unfortunately, the terminology is spreading so quickly, so fast, that I'm watching my work spin wildly out of control... as with all "telephone" whispers, sharing and gossip, my terminology from one single day was being turned into something completely different than what I'd actually taught.

And so I began this article. In order to prevent misunderstandings, incorrect deductions and incorrect terminology, I'm forced to share the most groundbreaking and healing discoveries of my work with you... One day I look forward to sharing my now famous seminars, *Past, Present & Future* as well as *Abstract vs. Swing* with you by DVD, but for now, this will have to do. I hope you will enjoy it as much as my attendees have.

The following are the most popular terms in use:

RENAISSANCE ERA

ren·ais·sance n.

a revival of <u>intellectual</u> or <u>artistic achievement</u> and <u>vigor</u>

West Coast Swing experienced what I call its "Renaissance Era" in the years around 1991-1999. Its waves lapped our shores before 1991 and left amazing treasures after 1999, but in general, our Renaissance occurred in the 90's. Never was there such a surge of "intellectual and artistic vigor" in our art form. During those years we saw the Great Minds of WCS, Country, Shag, Hand Dancing, Hustle and even Ballroom and Salsa converge, talk, share, teach, challenge and grow the dance. It's the Era that produced tapes which non-dancers in lunchrooms across America (and my inner-city classroom, by the way) were glued to when we played them. It's the Era when our Great Minds made breakthroughs in dance knowledge, technique and terminology that was and still is unparalleled in any other dance form. It's the Era which allowed, in Southern California alone, 12 studios (not including clubs!) to be dedicated to WCS and its sister dances. Some studios had full WCS classes every night of the week. It's the Era we lost to the digital age. It's the Era when we understood how hard WCS was to do, and we attracted dancers who were willing to work that hard to do it. It took five to seven years to learn WCS back then, and it was during the Renaissance that dancers applied for job transfers across multiple states to gain more training in WCS. It was during the Renaissance that dancers who had reached their peak in other dance forms became attracted to WCS because of its depth, difficulty and challenge. People dancing for two years called themselves beginners. It's the Era when audiences gave standing ovations before a routine was even done, and an Era when routines inspired you to jump out of your seat and move your feet!

PURE WEST COAST SWING

aka Renaissance Swing, Traditional WCS, Classic WCS or just... West Coast Swing

Pure West Coast Swing is the dance I outline in *West Coast Swing Essentials*. It has well over 35 elements. It takes years to learn. It is a highly connected lead and follow dance. The lead is center to center. Foot positions, body positions, control, and impeccable leading and following... they are of the utmost importance.

Pure WCS requires Timing, Technique and Teamwork (*The Three T's*), all of which are extremely high-end skills and none of which are easy. The body is always over one foot. It is not split weight. There is a leader and there is a follower. The leader is in charge of taking care of and leading his partner.

Pure WCS uses power points, body flight, triples, and subtleties that make you lean in and watch every second the better it is done. Pure WCS can be learned in a studio, has basic patterns and when a Novice learns it, they can dance with a Pure WCS Champion and feel like they've died and gone to heaven.

It's slotted. It has anchors. It's upright, tall and framed, but it is also grounded, into the floor and into the heels. It's easy to see when there's a mistake or a disconnect between the two partners. Pure WCS does not lend to 'cookie-cutter' partnerships, where everyone looks exactly like everyone else on the floor. WCS brings out a dancer's individuality, especially in its syncopations and stylings.

It's very easy to tell the difference between a novice, intermediate or advanced Pure WCS dancer. You can watch a floor and very quickly identify each level of dancer. In Pure WCS, the better a dancer becomes, the more they develop their own unique look. You can see their personality and style while they are doing the same exact basics as the newcomers. Each dancer has their own style, their own strengths, their own creativity, their own syncopations and the magic created when a unique lead draws a unique follow is like no other. There are numerous styles of Pure WCS because of its complicated nature, patterns and difficulty.

ABSTRACT IMPROVISATION

Abstract Improvisation is the other dance form we are seeing on the floor today. Because I have not written an article on it before, I will spend some more time outlining it here.

Abstract Improvisation's roots extend back 10 years ago. The roots grew very slowly in the beginning, but now, especially in the last three years, they've come into full bloom. In some so called "West Coast Swing" communities and clubs, it's the only dance they know. If asked to do an actual WCS pattern with triples and wraps, they would not be able to do so without great difficulty or without removing all of its footwork and timing.

I derived Abstract Improvisation's name from a combination of two terms: Abstract Art and Contact Improvisation. If you have not studied Abstract art or danced Contact Improvisation (two studies I would highly recommend), then here are some definitions of the two for you.

Abstract / Abstract Art
-difficult to understand
-a form of art with no rules, definition or boundaries
-a removal from reality
-form and line
-a period of art which followed the Renaissance

Contact Improvisation
-a form of modern dance improvisation
-points of physical contact provide the starting point for exploration through movement improvisation
-does not have rhythms, a step pattern, or music requirements

Touchdown Dance magazine once wrote the following about Contact Improvisation: "Contact Improvisation is a means to explore the physical forces imposed on the body by gravity, by the physics of momentum, falling and lifting. It is a complex but very open form with infinite possibilities and is a dance form that is made by the dancer in the moment of dancing." Keep this in mind, as it most definitely relates to Abstract Improvisation.

Abstract Improvisation has only four elements. It relies heavily on Teamwork but not Timing or Technique. It can be learned within a week to a month and does not require classes. It can be learned on the floor or on YouTube. It is highly improvised, *"made by the dancer in the moment of dancing,"* instead of being pattern based.

Dancers who do 'Abstract' look very much alike. It is almost impossible to tell the difference between a novice or advanced Abstract dancer beyond their differences in attitude, confidence and attire. Abstract leaders' feet are almost always wide and flat footed. In pictures their legs look like they are straddling a pony.

"Lines, shape and form" are created by straight, stretched arm leads and follows. Turns are led with rainbow arcs, high above the head, rather than halo turns, which leads to off balance following, which leads to arching backs and sways by the followers. The shoulders ride very high and the elbows are turned outside of the body, rather than tucked in towards the floor. The leads are less about leading her body, but more like "suggestions for direction." These "leads" are all in the arms leads, not body or center leads.

The footwork is not the focus in Abstract. The upper body *(waist, head, arms)* is where the action occurs. Your eyes are drawn towards the upper body area where spins are arching, hair is flying and arms look like they are holding giant beach balls. If you count to the music, and then look at the feet, you will find no relation. The feet are shuffling to catch the body, not drive the center. You will also notice how often single footed spins fall or gyrate off balance and the move is exited in an archway as a cover up.

Abstract isn't danced over the heel, but over the ball or flat foot. The feet are rarely turned out. Feet are used for catching falls, for straddling, for hitting lyrics and melodies, for sliding... not for holding a rhythm pattern, moving the body or leading. As a result, Abstract Improv can be danced over any kind of music- a waltz, a samba, a nightclub two step or a hustle. This is part of the reason that when a hustle or nightclub two step is played, dancers are still dancing what they call 'swing' on the floor, but only Abstract Improvisation works over any song.

Abstract Improv requires four elements: strong knees, a flexible spine, quick reflexes and total confidence. This is why young and untrained dancers excel at Abstract Improv. Their muscles don't injure as easily and they don't have years of training telling them to keep rhythms, posture, to lead correctly or to connect fully. Abstract Improv instruction often uses the following terms: *momentum, shape, channeling, improvisational, new school, flow, 3-D, free-styling, contemporary,* etc. Common Abstract phrases include *"the anchor is obsolete," "stretch out as far as you can go," "no leading, only suggesting," "there are no rules," "disconnect," "eliminate your triples," "split your weight across both feet," "dance behind the beat,"* etc.

When danced on beat, Abstract Improv is almost all single and double rhythm based and often the leader or follower can be seen standing in straddle position for well over four beats, while their upper half gyrates, sways or 'mimes' the lyrics.

The man does not post. The slot is often circular and free formed. The leader can move up and down the slot (or lack thereof), "flip-flop" positions with the follower and sometimes the follower is left in the middle while the leader dances around her. Pure WCS couples dancing next to an Abstract Improvisation couple will feel like they are being constantly run over or invaded by the Abstract couple's slot.

In Abstract Improvisation, major phrases are hit by tricks, swoops and falls that are dramatic but most often messy, as are they are done split weight, with loose high shoulders and extended lats.

Abstract Improvisation is not about controlled movement, but large, "sexy," or "on-the-floor" movements. Abstract dancers often replace the push break with a four beat 'push and pull,' and their Underarm Turn most often becomes a two beat "snap" by both partners to opposite ends of the slot.

Because of such quick movements, Abstract Improves seems much more big, bold and energetic than Pure WCS, and so Abstract dancers are put into finals instead of Pure WCS competitors, despite having a complete lack of timing, connection, technique or swing.

Yes, I said swing. Abstract Improvisation looks, feels and reflects many of the attributes of Contact Improvisation, which is a postmodern contemporary dance form, rather than any partner or rhythm based dance with steps, rules, leading and following. Therefore I classify Abstract Improvisation as a rudimentary contemporary dance (not to be confused with contemporary music), or modern dance. It's very similar to improvisational club dancing at young city nightclubs, but it is not a swing dance.

I've heard many times that Abstract Improvisation is really WCS "evolved." However, the world "evolved" connotes a movement towards a **higher** level of skill or movement. The fact that Abstract Improvisational dancers cannot do a series of WCS basics with critical timing, posture, centering, skilled leading or following, or any of the other incredibly difficult levels or patterns that Pure WCS demands, debates the idea of any "evolvement."

An elimination of excellent leading (*"we don't do 'prep prep' anymore"*), following (*"don't wait for me, you should do your own thing now"*), of centering, of foot positions, of syncopations, of timing… all of this only indicates a "devolvement" in my opinion, not an "evolvement." We would be wise to see these claims for what they really are: an excuse to keep students from going to any other instructor, to protect their own "revolutionary" brand, to gloss over training they don't have and to protect a dance that only *they* understand and therefore only *they* earn money off of.

Abstract Improvisation is such a far cry from Pure WCS, that the students of this new dance often find any other teacher's methods a threat. If they are at a convention and attend a Pure WCS instructors workshop, they will sometimes declare that they "only want to learn (fill in the blank: *"contemporary," "new school,"* etc, etc.) swing" and will sit the class out. And since Abstract Improvisation doesn't have any rules, students have walked away from conventions learning eight different ways to "anchor" or "replace their anchor," six different ways to hear the music, "feel it," "dance the emotion of it," "dance the lyrics," "dance the melodies," but never dance on beat, which is now, unfortunately, the rarest of finds at most conventions and many dance scenes across the country.

Let me clarify. To "dance on beat" refers to the dancer's feet dancing to the beat of the music. I often hear students and judges say that Abstract Improvisational dancers "hit every beat" in the music, when in reality, their upper bodies hit all of the breaks. This is actually pretty easy to do. What's *difficult* to do is lead and follow with your feet on beat AND hit the breaks. If you look at these "flashy" improvisational dancers' feet, you will suddenly see how very little skill is actually being executed.

The Time Has Come.

As you've probably figured out by now, I've discovered that we as a community now have two completely separate dances on our hands. I understand that this has been hard to see, especially since a handful of our top pros are able to do both depending on what music they are given, the audience they have, the judges they have, etc. But they comprise less than 1% of our community. And they've been dancing and teaching this new dance for a few years now, and we have been unaware of this shift. We've just seen the dancing change, but we didn't know how or why.

It is time to face reality. There are two dances.
It is time to admit the truth. There are two dances.
It is dangerous to deny it and stay on the path we are on.
And I mean **dangerous**.

First, it's dangerous physically, emotionally and mentally to our dancers. When a Pure WCS trained follower draws an Abstract Improvisation leader, she gets physically hurt by the clash. She feels totally lost and thinks she's in over her head. She is yanked off her anchor with no warning because Abstract Improvisation never moves on the same beat or even on a beat. She is put into precarious positions where she's not quite sure what's expected of her and gets hit in the head when trying to go down the slot.

When a Pure WCS trained leader draws an Abstract Improvisation follower, he can't figure out how to lead her, to connect with her, how to even get a push break out of her. She will be extremely light, to the point of complete disconnection or she will be extremely heavy and pull him off his anchor or timing. He will never ever get her on the foot he's trying to get her on, because she is not expecting him to lead her feet into positions.

It's the same the other way around. I'm hearing stories nearly every week about how an Abstract Improvisation leader draws a Pure WCS follower and accuses her of deliberately fighting him or getting in his way, when she is simply assuming he's doing the same dance. My inbox is jammed with horror stories of the meeting of these two dances on the floor. They are stories ranging from physical harm, to emotional harm to mental harm... and dancers are falling out of love with the dance. They just don't understand that there are two completely different dances on the floor today. Which brings me to my second point.

If we don't acknowledge that there are two dances, the future of the West Coast Swing industry is in jeopardy.

It's already suffering. Highly trained WCS professionals feel pressured to teach poor technique. Novice and intermediate dancers are suddenly instructors. Event directors are hiring unskilled teachers and dancers because they are cheaper and seem to be the "hot ticket" instead of hiring highly trained real WCS instructors. Classes are shrinking across America. Because Abstract Improvisation is just that, improvisational, and requires almost none of the skills and training that Pure WCS does, it doesn't have to be learned in a studio.

That doesn't mean there aren't people teaching Abstract Improvisation. There are. But people hear them say, in their so called "WCS" classes that, "we don't do that anymore, we do this now," and the students feel like they have to start all over in the dance. But the reality is that Abstract Improvisation really doesn't take any training. I'm meeting more and more dancers at conventions who have never taken a single WCS lesson and are having a blast.

In fact, Abstract Improv dancers, for reasons I've briefly touched on, make finals over Pure WCS dancers, which only promotes the idea to onlookers that classes, privates and lessons in general are not needed to be successful in the dance. Why spend money on Pure WCS, which absolutely has to be learned in a lesson setting and takes a long time to master, when you can learn Abstract Improvisation on YouTube for free? If we insist on calling Abstract Improvisation "Swing," then we are contradicting every single real WCS teacher out there and setting up all of their students for confusion, bitterness and failure. We will, ultimately, lose them. And then we will lose our instructors.

And then we will lose the dance.

We need to face facts. We need to remember what 'normal' is in the partner dancing communities. In healthier communities, like ballroom, the fact of the matter is that when someone has been learning a ballroom dance for three months and then dances with a ballroom pro, they feel like they are on top of the world and can do no wrong. It's like dancing with a dream. They are then are inspired to keep going, keep learning, keep expanding their knowledge and enjoyment of the dance.

But if a WCS dancer has been taking lessons for three months at a studio or a club and then asks a supposedly higher level dancer (because points tell them they are so, not other dancers) to dance, it will not be a pleasant experience. Those who have racked up points in the past five years are almost all Abstract Improvisational dancers, and they will completely run over this new beginner to our dance. The newcomer will be completely lost and feel defeated, not inspired. They will feel confused and torn. They will stick with lessons for about six months to a year and then they will give up, because they feel like they aren't getting any better.

In reality, they are learning one dance and yet asking someone who does a completely different dance to help them measure their progress. What a catastrophe for these dancers! It's heartbreaking, hearing their stories. Because we haven't admitted this other dance, our newcomers don't realize it's another dance that they're clashing with, never mind a lesser art form. And we should take a stand for them.

It is time, everybody.

People are done. People feel left behind. People feel ugly,

misunderstood, confused, angry and they feel scared. We are hemorrhaging veteran dancers at an astronomical rate, we are allowing our most talented individuals to feel "old" and we are attracting a demographic of dancers who would rather not work at their dancing because it's not "fun," and allowing instructors into our community who have absolutely no problem giving watered down shortcuts to technique, slandering our most knowledgeable and respected legends and calling an extremely difficult and praiseworthy dance "out of touch." Non-dancers have a better eye than we do now. Lunchrooms don't watch our videos after 2002. But they can't get enough of our Renaissance Era. They'll watch those tapes for hours.

It's time to put an end to the madness. It's time to equip our students, our fellow judges, our newcomers and our fellow dancers with the knowledge to walk into a studio, into a convention, into a workshop and say, "Okay, that's Abstract and that's Pure West Coast." And then they can make informed decisions. Then they can dance with freedom. Then they can understand what they're watching. Then they can understand what's going on...

And then we can heal.

Monday, September 19th 2011

An Affair to Remember
White Lights, City Nights

I do not live close to New York City. I live in a land where dancing was once heady, heavy, sexy and close knit. But it's not anymore. It's energetic, it's unique, it's socially connected... but it's not the dance Mecca that it once was. People drive less to dance less. People dance maybe once a week now, and if more, it's other dances... a salsa night here, a tango night there, a swing night in between. Gone are the euphorically addicting dances that kept me up nights and left me enamored and spinning with music and movement in my head... so much so that I made myself go to church on Saturday nights *before* dancing instead of Sunday mornings *after* dancing. After a night of dancing, Sunday mornings just didn't work. I just couldn't sit still. I couldn't listen... my feet were doing syncopations while the words of the sermon fought with the music and the leads and the dancing in my mind...

Now the word 'syncopation' is hardly used. And my dances have been slowly whittled away by poor leads... no, not poor leads... no leads. Or terrifying yanking at any random point. So I stay on the sides and watch the floor, waiting for the miraculous moment when I will see an opportunity for 1. a real swing song and 2. a real swing dancer, to actually become available at that one fine, glorious and golden moment. I don't care if I dance with a novice. I just want a darn swing dance. I get four a night if I'm incredibly lucky, but honestly, it's really down to one when I don't count my husband.

And then someone whispered in my ear: *Hudson Swing Affair!* Hudson Swing Affair? The one in New York? The one with the girls and tuxes and glamour? So I emailed Festa. And he told me the glorious news... no non-swing songs. Pure swing. And no competitions, which means the people there... must be there... for the dancing? only? Hmmm... sounds a little too good to be true. But it's Festa. And he's already too fabulous to be true. So. We prayed. We bought our tickets. We started to prepare as best we could. Gown and suit for the Black and White Ball? Check. Sturdy luggage? Check. Plenty of light clothing? Check. Curiosity in crazy amounts? Double check.

I'm so glad we went.

In fact, it hurt our hearts to leave. We left family behind. We left our hearts on the dance floor. Nick took me in his arms on the plane home and started to slow dance with me... suddenly I was back at the Pier Dance, with white lights surrounding me, a fabulous melody playing in my ears and the wind blowing gently through my hair. And I wish it was next year already.

If you ever traveled great distances to an event for the dances you could have, then you will be able to relate. My dances with Festa, Ramiro and Mark will stay with me forever, just as dances with them, Mark Eckstein, Demetre, Carlito and Mario and more, have stayed in my veins for years. They are the sustenance on which I live. They are the health food I crave. I never even missed the competitions. And I felt like I had a new home, like the Camelback Inn used to be for me. The sights and the heady and the sexy and the power and the strength of swing came crashing back upon me. People watched. People studied. People admired and they respected. They learned and they were inspired and they grew.

I don't know what the key ingredient is. Is it the lack of competitions? Is it the quality of staff? Is it the music? Is it the location? Is it Festa?

I suspect it's Festa. Because he maintains all the others. And his fans are loyal. And he treats them like the kings and the queens that they are. He is a lover of beauty. And beauty is everywhere you go at the Hudson Swing Affair.

And despite a bad flight there... a weak arrival at 2 am on Friday... and through a terrific scare with a supposed lost wallet... and needing to switch rooms at 5 am... even so... we ended up having the time of our lives.

My husband wasn't there when Kenny was around. My husband never went to the Camelback with me. My husband never saw the late night dancing sessions I still dream about... when I could trade off for four hours straight between dancers of such champion skill and control that I still shiver with edification, joy, expansion, growth and... 'yum' factors. Oh, the challenge and the real *dancing* that occurred then!

And oh the real dances I had at Hudson... with the exception of one single dancer there (from where I live, I guessed and of course, confirmed)... oh the *dances* I had... they were marvelous! And I'm glad beauty, goodness and swing are not gone forever... they are nestled in the bosom of the starry night that is… and I suspect will always be…

The Hudson Swing Affair.

The Weekly Notes

On Tuesday, October 11th of 2011, I began my series of Weekly WCS Notes. The goal was to release as much information as I could to my private list of followers without the hindrance of multiple drafts and re-writes I needed for public releases.

Though some of the Weekly Notes were eventually released to the public, most of them were not. The following are excerpts from my notes that I not only released to the public, but also put into .pdf format for studios, students and teachers across the world.

Monday, November 14th 2011

The Judging
How to Judge in Today's WCS Climate

I am a judge.
And I have sinned.

I was fooled by Abstract Improvisation. A couple of years ago, I left incredibly talented and highly trained and skilled Champion women out of finals. *"They aren't keeping up,"* I thought. *"What's wrong?"*

They were being hit on the head, yanked, dragged, discombobulated and seemed to move slower than their leaders. I looked over at other newer, younger girls, who never batted an eye at their leaders. They just dipped, twirled and whirled with a big smile on their face. They flew around like the end of a lasso with seeming ease.

So I put the new girls in.

I am so sorry. I knew not what I did. I know so much more now.

My eyes were used to judging on those who "gelled" with their partners... those who had "seamless" dances. I didn't realize things had changed so much that is was time to watch for much more than that... no matter what the level.

The reality of what I saw: the clash of two dances. The Champion WCS women were trying to stay on time, trying to follow, trying to stay in a slot. This spelled disaster with their Abstract men, who needed them to do *anything* but those three things.

And as a result, the Abstract women, who in reality were up high on their tippy toes, knees bent, tushies out, shoulders riding up to their ears, running around split weight, off time, pigeon toed and so uncontrolled that their man's poor leads never showed in their bodies... looked unruffled. And thus looked... successful.

How wrong I was. I eliminated the most highly trained and skilled dancers on the floor that day... because they tried to do West Coast Swing.

I judge very differently nowadays.
Times have changed,
and therefore our judging needs to change.

The days of judging on the Three T's are gone. They work great when people are doing Pure WCS, or any other pattern and footwork based dance for that matter. But nowadays when I'm judging a "swing" contest, less than 10% are dancing "swing."

At Boogie by the Bay I watched two heats of Novice, with 40 couples in each heat, I saw ONE man lead West Coast Swing consistently. That's 1 in 80 novice men. I saw a number of followers trying to do swing, but their partners did not take kindly to them, unfortunately. I hope I missed some real WCS men. I really really do. I know Abstract is not so dominant in other areas of the country, but still, I haven't seen a floor where it isn't present to one degree or another.

So how do I judge now? I watch everyone's feet. In every division. It reveals everything. And I mean everything. Try it sometime. You'll be amazed. And then, as I watch the feet, I look for the following things in the following order.

THE NEW JUDGING METHOD

1) Look for anyone dancing real West Coast Swing.

If a leader is leading West Coast Swing, I put him in. If the follower is trying her best to do West Coast Swing, no matter what kind of lead she gets, I put her in. The couples in finals that actually do West Coast Swing... they are automatically in my top five. Everyone doing West Coast Swing has first priority. No matter what level.

How do I judge the WCS dancers against each other? It rarely happens anymore on the competitive circuit. I've seen in a few times in local clubs though. And when I see 2 or more couples clearly doing WCS, then I used the typical method: The Three T's: Timing, Technique and Teamwork...

Anyone who judged during our Renaissance Era and earlier will find this easy, almost instinctive. Judging dancers doing the same dance is always easier. One day in the future, if a miracle occurs and there are two or more Pure WCS dances that have those Three T's, THEN I go into Difficulty, Showmanship, etc.

We judges with training tend to assume dancers have the Three T's, especially in the upper levels, and then judge on difficulty (part of the reason rushed dips and tricks win), but we've forgotten that doing the Three T's right in Pure WCS is MUCH harder than any sloppy trick. Just ask my partner Josh. He has had to put in A LOT of hard work, even today... to dance WCS well when most of his peers are doing Abstract Improvisation.

As such, event directors and dance professionals outside of WCS have begun commenting on how amazing Josh is now dancing. But his "all-star" followers are furious. They can't dance with him. They don't know how. And the "all-star" leaders keep asking me what he's doing differently, because his pictures suddenly look so amazing when theirs don't. It's a crazy world out there. It's time to award real swing above all else, and the Abstract dancers will learn it's time to catch up.

2) Look for anyone who is dancing ON TIME.

After placing and ranking all my WCS dancers, I move on to who is actually ON TIME. Not ahead of it, not before it, but ON the beat of the music. I look at the dancer's feet, and if the leader is actually being purposeful with his feet and the beat of the music, then I put him higher than the men shuffling their feet randomly. Same with the women. If they are keeping their feet in accordance with the music rather than completely ignoring it, then I put them in under the WCS dancers, even if the WCS dancers aren't as tight with their timing.

Now here's the key. When I say "on-time," I'm referring to the beat of the music, not the lyrics or the melodies. So many teachers are telling students that being "on time" is dancing to the lyrics, the melodies or something other than the BEAT. That's ridiculous in any lead and follow dance, not just WCS. So I'm looking for a dancers' relation to the beat, whether it's an obvious rhythm or not.

A quick tip is to start counting the music, "& a 1, & a 2, & a 3" BEFORE looking at a dancers' feet, then keep counting, and THEN look at their feet. Too many judges try to do both at the same time and starting counting to the feet rather than the music. Don't fall into that trap.

Now, if you see their feet actually wait for the '1' to do a weight change, etc, etc, then I can start to rank them. Abstract dancers look effortless from the waist up because they are hitting breaks in the music 'upstairs' while completely ignoring the music's beat with their feet downstairs. Look down, not up, to see the real story, and your judging will become much easier.

Another popular trick is to start the dance on time with their partner... say, for the first 16 beats, and then they go nuts afterwards. This is so confusing for the real WCS dancers. They think they understand what's going on, and then all of a sudden the dancing goes into random lyrical or club wanderings. I only place those who stay on beat throughout the whole dance, not part of it.

This goes for routines too. Because dancers are getting choreography from more than one source, I watch their routine switch between on beat patterns and then suddenly dance as if there is no beat, and then switch back. It hurts my brain. And leaves the audience stilted and confused. I'm looking for an entire dance to be on beat, not just part.

3) Look for body control (dance technique and training).

More and more I'm hearing stories that the trained female dancers left on our competition floors are being told to "dirty up" their dancing and to stop being so "controlled." They are literally being "shamed" into messy dancing.

The other term I'm hearing a lot these days is "great energy." "I'm looking for the dancers who have great energy out there," I'll hear a judge say. I'll ask them to point out who they think exhibits great energy, and they will point to the sloppiest, craziest and most flamboyant dancer on the floor. The one that clearly doesn't know what they are doing, who could care less what their partner is doing and who is clearly unaware of that little thing called training.

"I'm just here to have fun," these dancers say. Fun? Have fun on the social floor. Not on the competition floor. Not unless your idea of fun is dancing well and with your partner. The very definition of "dance competition" is the idea of who can dance better than anyone else on the floor. It's not about who can goof off more than anyone on the floor... it's a DANCE competition, not a fool and flagrant competition. No wonder injuries are knocking out dancers for six months to a year.

Anyone off the street can be fun, wiggle and get wild... but fun can't be practiced, it can't be taught in a class and it should never be rewarded in an actual dance competition.

Training and control is essential. You can't be a good leader if you aren't controlled. You can't be a good follower if you aren't controlled. You can't create, can't grow, can't expand without growth of skill... and that all amounts to how much control we have over our bodies. I look for dancers who are purposeful with their movements. If they stand tall with their shoulders down and back, their butt tucked underneath their bodies, dancing over one foot vs. split weight, then I promise you, they'll stand out on the floor.

Forget the dancers they say have "energy," when in fact it means a little crazed and frantic. This is a dance competition. And a good dancer is nothing without control... so much control that one flick of a finger is more powerful and eye-catching than any booty shake.

4) Look for who is leading and following.

Is the man actually looking at his partner and leading her? Is the girl really trying to follow the man? I hate judging Abstract Improvisation, but there are some who actually lead it and some who actually follow it. It is so important to start emphasizing lead and follow once more. I watch for body leads instead of arm leads. I'm looking for attentive leaders and attentive followers. And by attentive, I don't mean they are looking each other in the eye... I mean they are looking where they are going, paying attention to each other's centers, trying to be in-sync with their partners.

5) Look for real dancing.

When I have to scrape the barrel and put people in I really don't want to, I look for those who are at least "trying" to dance with their partner, instead of the ones who are simply performing for themselves out there. I never place those who compete for themselves. Nissies don't make great partners on the floor... a humble spirit is always a plus on the dance floor.

6) Don't worry about violations.

A violation literally holds NO weight in our judging system. It doesn't change one's placement, ranking or points. But it does put a target on the judges' back, or makes the couples and competitors confused. I can't think of a single reason to violate anyone when it doesn't do anything at all. I say everything in my scores.

In 2009 seven out of the ten finalists in the US Open Classic Division were violated for swing content. Seven out of ten! But all the dancers who weren't violated were placed *at the bottom* of the scoreboard. How ridiculous is this? It's a *SWING* competition! Swing is right their in the event's name: The US

Open SWING Dance Championships. You'd expect the swing routines to be at the top of the scores, not the bottom. But violations give judges an excuse to skip that little piece of logic. So when it comes to violations, don't worry about them. This judging system makes them irrelevant.

What about 'flash and trash'?

When I see a lot of dipping, dropping and sliding, I've noticed that it's always by Abstract dancers that don't have any of the skills I just listed. It's time to start seeing these flashy moves as a red flag rather than a sign of success. These slides, slips and tricks have hurt so many women, even the professionals, because they are no longer done with control or technique.

These tricks are never really led, never mind being led on beat. It's only the girls who are uncontrolled enough to be thrown around that succeed in these moves. And when pictures are taken, the chaos is revealed. Shoulders high, feet splayed, pigeon toes, crunched necks... not long, lovely or powerful lines. Audiences will cheer when a follower slips and slides randomly on her knees, **but our scores are supposed to reflect success, not mess.**

Sadly, all of the champion women I judged a few years ago have all left the competition floor. I can't say that I blame them, but I will never forget that I played a part in that loss. I strongly urge you to start judging as if the Three T's are automatically in existence. They aren't. Be aware of the two dances, be aware of the difference between a charming, funny dancer and a good one, and don't let the scores of other judges affect your own.

Be a good *judge*, not a good *politician*.

We have lost almost all of our talent in the upper levels. Let's not lose the new talent coming into the dance... and let's let our competitors know that we're looked for GOOD DANCING again, not BIG DANCING.

The "New" Etiquette

The New Rules to Survive Today's Dance Floor

There are some solid rules of etiquette that most of us have been trained in and live by on the social dance floor... for decades.

Examples?

- Always say "yes" when someone asks you to dance.
- If you have to turn someone down because you're resting, in the middle of a conversation or are otherwise "indisposed," then be sure to catch them on the next song.
- Establish your slot at the start of the dance and stay in it.
- Acknowledge the spouse when asking their partner.
- If you sweat profusely, bring a change of top.
- Don't eat garlic or onions before you go social dancing...

The list goes on and on... and yet most of us can't remember where we first learned them. We just know they exist, and we do our best to adhere to them. These rules have helped new dancers become better, helped keep our dance environment polite, civil and in reality, quite positive. These rules are held, by many of us, to be both holy and universally known.

I was blessed to start dancing swing, ballroom and country western when these rules were being followed by the entire dance community. Those who didn't were branded as the local meanie or snob and were pointed out to newcomers as the ones to be wary of.

But when I fell hopelessly in love with West Coast Swing and immersed myself in that particular swing scene, I learned a whole new level of etiquette. The men made sure every single lady was walked to their car. Doors were opened for the women and jeans were snubbed as a "dishonor to the dance." The level of etiquette was so high, in fact, that my own husband had to meet with the men in my community to find out what I was used to.

But those days are behind us.

Things have most definitely changed. In a lot of ways. And as such, it can be downright dangerous to follow these rules as we once did. I have said "it's time" to acknowledge that there are Two Dances being danced on the West Coast Swing scene, and now I'm also saying that "it's time" to instate a new etiquette.

THE "NEW" ETIQUETTE

Some rules still apply. It's still rude to ignore another's spouse. It's still polite to avoid onions, garlic and even heavy perfumes before heading to the social dance floor. But some rules most definitely don't apply anymore.

New Rule #1:
Don't assume anyone knows the rules.

I've worked as a private contractor for a number of small businesses. The number one issue they faced when it came to problems with internal and external customer service was the generational issue. Older generations believed the younger generations knew certain rules and chose to ignore them. But they most often just needed to be told. Nearly 99% of the workforce problems were solved at the companies I worked with when expectations were clearly spelled out to the younger generation. Even simple ones, like 'greet a customer when they walk in the door,' and 'save personal computer use for your break.'

Don't expect that your rules of common dance decency are known to anyone else. I'm constantly meeting students who are being driven nuts by people who are blatantly ignoring common etiquette. And I tell them... they may not know the rules. Of course, once the rule breakers learn them, they should be held to account. There's no excuse for *conscious* rude behavior. Be aware and be prepared. Not everyone is on the same page concerning etiquette.

New Rule #2:
DO NOT, under ANY circumstances "help" your partner!

This used to be an unspoken rule, but man, oh, man, have people forgotten it! This rule has been broken in dance classes, in workshops, on the social dance floor and even (seriously?) on the competition floor.

NO. There is absolutely NO excuse to give, as you all love to call it, "feedback" on the dance floor. Okay, fine, there is one exception... and ONLY one: "That hurts." Again, this is about injury... if you are being pushed, pulled, yanked, tweaked, squeezed or if your hair gets caught in a wristband, etc, etc, etc... by all means, say something.

But that's it. And I mean, that's IT.

DO NOT 'help' your partner. DO NOT 'assist' the teacher while rotating. DO NOT 'show' your partner the correct way... do not, do not, do not! offer any unsolicited help, advice or commentary.

Do I have a multitude of stories for you! A million gazillion. Shoot, I even heard that a guy lifted a girls' chin and told her to "look him in the eyes" while she danced with him. Really??? How invading is that? He touched her chin? In order to do something other than leading? And then told her to look in his eyes? Are you kidding? And the worst part is, she was a champion dancer... and was not dancing with her equal. At all. I am consistently shocked at the boundaries that are being crossed out there. Sigh.

Can you tell? This is an extremely upsetting trend for me, and I have to say, from what I've seen and heard, it's a rampant one.

We have become obsessed,
to the detriment of our community,
with ignoring "our side of the street,"
and looking over at "their side of the street"
to see what needs "fixing."

If you have ever ever *ever* offered unsolicited commentary, then I'm sorry, but YOU have a lot to fix on your own side of the street. Work hard to become the best leader, the best follower and the best dancer you can be... and STOP trying to help anyone else get there. Every teacher I have talked to says that they people who 'help' in class are always the absolute *last* person anyone should be listened to. That's been my experience too. The people who actually know what they are doing... they are *listening* in class, not teaching others. It's an incredibly frustrating trend for those of us who have been teaching for decades.

As such, those of you who find yourself trapped with a "helper," whether it's social dancing or in class, do not encourage them and do not heed their advice. I've heard the worst techniques and tips shared on the social floor (usually an Abstract dancer trying to change a Swing dancer). It's rude behavior, and anyone who is rude is not worth listening to. Just keep going, wait out the advice, say "I'm okay," or "I hear what you're saying," when they press you for a response, and please... please, please, please, do not thank them for the help! and **never** say you're sorry. The uber-nice tend to immediately apologize a lot. Helpers love this... they feed on it. And they will only come after you more because of it.

Spare a life, encourage joy and happiness on the floor, and blissfully ignore the "helpful" words of the truly unhelpful dancers.

New Rule #3:
Never demand a dance.

I can't believe I'm even saying this, but apparently this is a much needed rule... you wouldn't believe the stories I hear. Ladies... if there is an excellent lead in the room who is actually willing to share his talent with all of the rest of the ladies, then show him some respect. Apparently women are cursing, throwing tantrums and fighting with the leads when they say that they have a line waiting. Men... just because you gathered up the courage to ask, does not mean she owes you something. You are also throwing fits, arrogance and obscenities. This behavior baffles me.

Ladies and gentleman!
When you **ASK** somebody to dance,
then you are open to hearing either a "yes," OR a "no" in reply.
Anything less, and you are **DEMANDING** a dance.

And that, everyone, is just plain out of line and rude. Never, ever demand a dance. This is not the way to get someone to dance with you. If a man is ever ugly when I turn them down, I certainly do not intend to reward that behavior by actually saying "yes" to them ever again. There is no rule, nor has there ever been a rule, that you deserve a dance before anyone else or at the exact moment you ask for it.

There is only one exception: the spouse. The spouse trumps all. If 'he put a ring on it,' then that lady and/or man gets first dibs, no matter what the line is for their partner.

My husband has seen the worst of this, and so has my partner Josh. They are "the nice guys," and for some reason this gives the ladies the freedom to abuse them somehow. And that's when I see the ugliness... when I dare to ask my husband for a dance. Oh dear, the ladies do lose it! But according to the boys, the ladies are starting to lose it no matter what. They are even asking three or four times a night, no matter how exhausted the men are or how many ladies are waiting.

What's going on? **Never demand a dance.** Oh... you can run helter skelter across a floor to get to a favorite first, but be gracious *no matter what answer* you receive.

New Rule #4:
Do not videotape anyone without permission.

The issue of videotaping is one I'm blatantly stealing from Kelly Casanova. But it's necessary. Unconstrained videotaping of everyone and anyone, every where and every place, is widespread in our community. This is a new problem. Yes, I said *problem.*

Just because you can videotape, doesn't mean you should. Witness Protection has had to relocate dancers because a video was posted of them at a dance on YouTube without their knowledge. Teachers are losing income and leaving the dance because students are taping them socially or during class in order to steal moves for other teachers or avoid paying for the class themselves. The list goes on and on...

As with so much in life, **just because you can, doesn't make it right**. Get a person's permission before filming, INCLUDING the people in the background of your video. And don't be surprised if a pro walks off the floor when you start filming them. It's incredibly rude, invasive and selfish.

So when it comes to videotaping, just be aware, okay? And for those of you who teach, write up some ground rules for videotaping in your class. For example, I don't allow my classes or workshops to be filmed, but I do allow people to film my husband and I dancing a move at the end of class. Sometimes I offer the counts and sometimes I don't. Sometimes I dance it to music and sometimes I don't. It depends on where I am and what kind of students I have, etc. I am very conscious of what I do on film. I can deal with people videotaping for personal use, especially when I travel so often, but I'm very aware of how valuable such an offering is.

It's a serious gift for any pro to allow their work to be videotaped. It's our product, it's our living and we're giving it away for free. Students pay for the workshop, not the 'video notebook.' It lends to less privates, less paid hours, less income and more competition. Frankly, I'm amazed when students believe we pros are "obligated" to put our product on film. No. It's actually a big favor. And for those of us who are extremely talented teachers, it's a HUGE favor.

Back in the day, if you wanted the move you just learned on film, you went out into the hall and danced it yourself while someone filmed you. There's nothing wrong with that. Having a pro dance it for you, especially with counts and tips? That's a huge gift, so respect it, honor it, and don't complain when they choose not to film, and definitely don't share the video when they do. Yes? Yes.

New Rule #5:
Ask a pro or champion only once a weekend.

The rule used to be that you could ask your pro or champion only once a night. But fewer pros and champions are out dancing, and many more dancers are being extremely pushy about getting a dance *(see Rule #3)*. So when you know a pro or a champion that is out and willing to dance... take it as chance for a free private lesson... and dance with them once, and *only once*, for the entire weekend.

We professionals do talk, you know, and when someone abuses the 'once a night' rule at a convention, or over a weekend, and asks every single night. That's really pushing it. Some of you even ask for help or lessons on the floor. And then we remember you... but not in a good way. If we ask you, then hey, you're super lucky. Rock it out. But in the meantime, be pleased with your one dance. You can learn so much from it. And it will keep that pro and/or champion from only dancing with their students or staying in their room for the rest of the night.

New Rule #6:
Feel free to wait for the right song.

You might already be doing this, because I've learned this trick from watching others. If you want to dance swing with a partner, wait for a swing song. I've seen both leads and follows just say, "Yes, but not to this song." And then they both meet up later and dance together.

That's just a really smart approach to dancing for both of you. No one loses out. If it doesn't make you want to do swing, then the dance simply won't do either one of you justice. And you will have a harder time learning the dance or even getting better at it if you dance to inappropriate music for it too much. Degrading music degrades your dancing. Waiting for a song that naturally works for WCS only leads to better dancing on everyone's part, assuming you're both WCS trained.

People love hearing yes, and when you want to wait because of the song, they know you're not waiting because of themselves as a partner. I've never seen a bad reaction to this request yet. Just do it if you want to. DO NOT use it as a way to say no. That's passive aggressive. Be honest with your boundaries and mean what you say. Everyone deserves at least that amount of respect.

And, by the way, feel free to start requesting songs from the DJ's. How do you think all the DJ's have the "new" music that they are playing? Most of them are requested by the Abstract dancers. So start requesting your favorite swing song. You'll be glad you did! And a tip in their tip jar helps even more, of course.

New Rule #7:
Avoid Nissies.

Partner dancing doesn't work unless you have respect for your partner. Nissies see their partner as someone to "use." They use you as an excuse to take the front row, to be seen, to show themselves off, to declare judgment on you... they only "use."

I watched one Abstract Nissy dance right in front of a girl having her birthday dance. The crowd wanted to cheer for the girl, but they were so uncomfortable that the guy just went up there and blocked our view of her, that we were all just silent. I wasn't hosting the dance, so I didn't have the willpower to take over and yank him off the floor *(ohhhhh, how I wish I had!),* but as soon he was done with his partner, he came and asked me to dance with him, before the birthday dance for this girl was over.

I smiled and gave a very firm "No thanks." I will not dance in front of someone else on their birthday dance. I will not say "yes" to a leader who very clearly just wants to seen and requires me to be yanked, thrown and diminished in order to prove he's "better" when he's really just an intermediate dancer (at best.) He didn't want to dance "with" me. He wanted to dance "over" me in front of everyone when they were sitting out in respect to the birthday girl. Why bother? Who in the world signs up for that when they join their first dance class?

Remember. Just because a guy or girl in your neck of the woods has "points" and lords it over you, doesn't mean that they are a better dancer than you anymore. It just means, in most cases, that they have more attitude or arrogance than you, and that they find you disposable as a partner.

Attitude doesn't make for a good dance. Nissies only feed their ego when you dance with them. If they have no one to dance with, they have no one to abuse. Let them dance with each other or go dance somewhere else. Nissies have NO edifying value in any community... they only destroy. It's very subtle, sometimes not so subtle, but you can do you part by refusing to 'feed their need.' And you'll spare yourself an enormous amount of pain and confusion in the process.

New Rule #8:
Learn to be okay saying "no."

I used to say yes to everyone, even after I became a champion. I was known for it. I loved dancing, and I never hesitated to just say... "YES!" No matter who they were. When I run into dancers I haven't seen in decades they say, "oh, you... you used to dance with, used to dance with... well, everyone!"

But today? I'm VERY good at saying "No, thank you." It's never comfortable for me. It's always difficult. But it's very necessary. Especially when it comes to my bodily protection. And it's essential that you learn the skill as well.

There are times when you are in harms way. And you need to know when those times come and act accordingly. There are two dances, and as I've said a million-jillion times before... it's painful mentally, physically and emotionally when these two dances clash on the floor. Women and men all over California have dislocated shoulders, necks and hips from being "nice" and saying "yes" to Abstract dancers who could care less about taking care of their partner.

Men watch in shock and horror as the women they are dancing with decide to lean... lean... leeeeeaaaaan... and face plant themselves on the floor. Pulling their leaders down with them. And then turning and saying, "Wasn't that cool?" I have now seen this happen on both coasts in America and I have *never* heard the guy say, "Yeah, that was cool." It makes the man look like he dropped her, and it makes the man fall and often injured. Both men and women have sustained injuries that have kept them off the dance floor from 6 months to three years. There is nothing okay about this.

The second part to this rule? If you say "yes," and discover they are doing a different dance, you don't have to lie and pretend like you're having fun. I'm shocked at how many skilled women feel like they have to make a bad lead feel "good" about themselves. I'm not saying to stare them down, but back in the day, we would watch each other to see if we were enjoying the lead and/or follow we were getting. But now, we all seem to be working hard at lying to each other and saying we're having a ball, even when we're not. This is especially true with the ladies... the ladies of today are in full "nurture" mode... they are on a mission to make the guy feel good... even when the guy is making them feel very very bad.

This helps no one. It makes the men think they are perfect and don't need work, and it makes the women forget what a good lead feels like. I'm not advocating rude behavior. **I'm advocating honesty**. Don't make the effort to be radiant all the time unless your partner is actually interested in giving you a good dance. You don't need to have a sour look on your face... I'm not saying that at all. But I'm careful to only say it was wonderful when, well, it was actually wonderful.

To this day I am still happy to say "yes" to all levels of swing dancers. But it has cost me greatly, especially as an instructor. I've had to stop by gas stations on the way home to get ice for my hand, my foot, a knee or a shoulder. This is astonishing, and absolutely not okay. So I've found it necessary to be increasingly wary.

One dancer in Northern California was so polite when he first started asking me. He was a joy to dance with. But then he stopped taking lessons and started gripping my hand so hard with his thumbs that, despite my requests to let go, I'd end up icing my hands for three days, making my job painful and sometimes impossible. I was very honest with him. I told him this repeatedly, and he just did not care. He squeezed harder than ever. As if to prove a point.

So I had to start turning him down. He was completely unwilling to believe he was causing the massive bruising on my hands, and so... we had to part ways. I still had a hard time saying no, but it was most definitely worth it. Anytime your partner puts their ego above your physical well being it not worth stepping onto the floor with.

Another dancer, years ago, wanted to do a Classic routine with me. He even went so far as to tell others we were partnering, even when we weren't, to prevent anyone else for asking me. Other professionals were pushing me to dance with him and some were even mad that I never did. I was being pushed from every direction to dance with this man.

But what no one knew, was that during one of our very first practice sessions, he did a move that literally threw my across the floor on my back. We're talking more than ten feet across the floor… it was a hard smack followed by a long skid. I looked up at him in horror wondering what in the world had happened. And do you know what he was doing? He was laughing. And laughing hard. And he said, with this proud smirk, "I thought that would happen."

That was it. I didn't say anything, but I never set up another practice session with him again, and I knew I would never agree to dance with him. My only sorrow, looking back, was that I never told anyone this. I just listened in silence as I was pushed from eight different sides to dance with this man, that I knew I could never trust my physical well being with.

And that was back when we were both doing WCS. I know some current professionals who are willing to put up with this dangerous behavior, just to keep dancing in the Top 5. It makes me so upset when I walk by them practicing and one partner is being incredibly abusive to the other partner… and they just take it. Willingly. You can see that it's a choice. But they have paid for it physically.

My point is that no one is immune. Newcomers to advanced dancers to professionals… we all have a responsibility to ourselves to go into anything, a social dance, a strictly swing or a routine with eyes wide open. And all of us have the freedom, right and justification to say no at certain times. I repeat:

This rule is not about dance experience or levels. It is about different goals, different dances, health and protection.

Be comfortable saying "No, thank you" when it comes to your mental, emotional and physical well being. No matter who you are and what kind of dancing you're doing.

And so there you go... new rules to live by. The biggest one of all is having the freedom to say "no," in my opinion. Again, it's not easy, but then again, neither is becoming injured. When I say "no" I always say it with a smile and I always, always, always just say "No," or "No, thank you!" Never say more than that.

Unless, of course, you really are just looking to dance with them later. If I tell a guy "no" because I really am hurting or tired, I actually tell them that. I clearly state, "I need to sit out a dance to rest, but I'll be sure to catch you next." And that's exactly what I do. Ask around. The only time I say "no" and nothing else is when I don't want to be asked by them again.

It's imperative that we be choosy nowadays. Not everyone is out for a "good dance" with their partner. Not everyone is interested in being a good lead or a good follow. So get educated. Choose wisely. And become comfortable with the word "no" when you need to.

Put all these new rules into play, and you'll start enjoying your dancing a whole lot more- and your reputation will improve as well. "Knowing is half the battle," as they say, and now you know.

Now, go enjoy the dance floor like never before!

The Tenets of Swing
The Tenets of All Swing Dances

The saying "swing is swing" has wreaked some havoc on our community. I have no idea why, but it has been used to wipe out any definition of swing whatsoever lately. So when I heard it used to justify the refusal to violate anyone on swing content at a major event a few years ago, it made me wonder...

Exactly what IS swing?

I don't just mean West Coast Swing. I outlined those characteristics in Swing Essentials a while ago. I mean, what is it that makes a dance a "swing" dance, instead of a Latin, Smooth or Folk dance? I began thinking. I began studying. And I thought about all forms of swing... Balboa, Shag, Lindy, East Coast, West Coast... all of them.

And the more I studied, watched, discussed and learned, the more settled I became upon the following points below. I call them The Tenets of Swing©.

THE TENETS OF SWING

TENET #1:
All Swing Dances are Lead and Follow Based.

All swing patterns, no matter what form of swing you're dancing, require a leader who decides what moves take place and when, and a follower, who is responsible for following these leads. It may sound obvious, but a slew of teachers worldwide are telling students to "improvise" and "suggest" instead of actually leading and following, and that personal innovation, musicality and emotion overrides connection, frame, etc, the things required for both leading and following.

In reality, all swing dances have basic patterns, basic figures and all of the more difficult patterns are completely based upon the basic patterns. All the patterns have steps for the leader and steps for the follower. Even during syncopations, the leader or the follower is in sync with their partner and music. There is no such thing as "freestyling" or pure improvisation in any of the swing dances.

TENET #2:
In All Swing Dances, the Follower Orbits the Leader.

Different styles of swing have different types of orbits. Some have a circular orbit, some have a slotted orbit and some orbit in a nice tiny square. But any way you slice it, the man navigates the follower around himself in some form of an orbit.

In contrast, other dances have the two dancers moving around the entire room in a big circle. Both partners go down the "line of dance." In other dances, the partner switch places. The leader starts on point A and the follower starts on point B. During the move or by the end of the move, they have switched places. The leader is now on point B and the follower is now on point A.

But all swing dances are different than this. The leader is in the center of the circle or slot, and the follower joins him, passes him or goes around him. She "orbits" him. You can check my YouTube Channel for a video example of these orbits throughout a variety of swing dances.

TENET #3:
All Swing Dances Have Extremely Fast Feet.

Rock steps, kicks, heel-toe action, shuffles, slides... oh my! You'll never see anyone call swing dancers "lethargic" will you? All the swing dances have quite a bit of energy, because they all require more footwork than the average partner dance.

Every swing style has a totally different set of footwork, but none of the styles are without it. If you have studied any of the ballroom dances, you'll know that they are all almost exclusively comprised of single and double rhythms. Not so with the swing dances. On the whole they are comprised of rather complicated rhythms like triples and quads. When it comes to swing dances, the dancers are relatively still on top and active on the bottom. In swing, it's the feet that do the talking.

The Rock Step

I do want to make a special note of one particular step: the Rock Step. There is not one single swing dance that does not have a Rock Step in their patterns at least once. Shag, Balboa, WCS, ECS and Lindy... watch an entire dance and you'll see at least one Rock Step from both the leaders and followers, if not more. Rock, rock, rock around the clock! Rock steps are an essential part of ALL swing dances. Without them, we become something else... and it sure ain't swing.

TENET #4:
All Swing Dances are POSITIVE!

I've said it before and I'll say it again: swing music, no matter what style you're dancing, will make you "check in." It makes you come alive instead. It gets you off the couch. It makes you want to live. To expand. To get out of your seat!

Some forms of swing celebrate passion and some forms of swing celebrate life... but either way, it makes you feel brighter. It highlights the good things in life. It's not dark. It's not depressing. It's not degrading and it's most definitely not designed to make you "chill," "check out," or "lay back." Swing does the opposite.

And there are the Swing Tenets. The more I study our history and watch our videos, I can see them all... over and over again... throughout the decades.

We are a passionate people, we swing dancers. But I believe that true swing dancing brings out the best in us... and when it brings out the worst, then perhaps the dance has lost its way.

Let's start listening to our music again, and seeing if it really makes us want to live, to expand, to grow and to move... and let's look down at our feet and rediscover what they are made for... and let's rediscover the joy of true leading and true following. Let's rediscover...

SWING!

The UKWCSDTA

On Tuesday, April 11*th* 2012, I was contacted by Mike Rosa, a WCS instructor and promoter based out of the UK. I learned about the UK West Coast Swing Dance Teachers Association for the first time. I was asked to be an Honorary Director and Contributor.

Of course, I gladly agreed, but upon hearing about the organization's efforts to develop a WCS teacher certification program, I was also inspired. And so I wrote the following article specifically for the UKWCSDTA. In fact, anyone teaching partner dancing, in my opinion, should have the training to meet the following requirements. Of course, they are wonderfully helpful skills to obtain even as a student. Enjoy…

Monday, May 7ᵗʰ 2011

To Be a Teacher
The Minimum Requirements Before Handing Out Your Card

Partner dancing is a complicated art. No matter what form of it you are doing, you are essentially bringing two separate people, with their own physical, mental and emotional strengths, gifts and weaknesses... **together.** And they must trust one another. One must trust him to lead. One must trust her to follow. And both must trust each other to dance in sync with the music.

And so, as in marriage, partner dancing can bring out the best and the worst in us. As all that we are unfolds in the arms of another on the dance floor, so must the teacher be aware of this delicate situation. And that's just the start.

When it comes to teaching partner dancing, in this case West Coast Swing – What makes someone eligible to teach? In an ever increasing self-promoting society, where people will hand you "their card" within a month of learning the dance, it's becoming more and more important to know what the requirements are for prospective instructors. What makes them worth investing your money and your time with? Just because someone says they are a teacher, or starts a class, doesn't mean they should be teaching or should be gathering students to them.

It is now in the hands of students, clubs and organizational leaderships to evaluate and determine who is truly worthy of the title "Dance Instructor." The following are the minimum standards that I believe every teacher who is worth an hour of anyone's time must meet:

1. An instructor should be able to chart and phrase music.

Well trained aerobic instructors are required to understand the music they are playing for their classes. It is a well known and accepted practice. Since partner dancing generally requires a much more diverse library of music, it makes charting the necessity of this skill for any dance teachers' training even more important.

Dance teachers should be able to chart and phrase both 3/4 music as well at 4/4 music, and must understand the "dancers count" instead of the "measures" that musicians use. They must understand the difference between the 1 and the 5 in 4/4 music and they must understand that the mini-phrase in 3/4 music is not 3 beats long, but 6 beats long, etc. They must know the difference between the mini-phrase and the major phrase, and must understand how to chart bridges, etc. I have seen numerous ways to chart music, and though I love my current method, I have never seen the other methods steer anyone wrong. A teacher should choose their method wisely, and then learn it well.

This ability to "chart" music is essential for every teacher who is in charge of bringing the music to light for students who are in the position of leading or following. Even if they don't train the students in phrasing themselves, the mere knowledge of it lends to better instruction... from waiting for the intro of a song to pass before starting the call of a pattern, to ensuring they "finish" the complete phrasing of a pattern, instead of leaving the students half-way through a step, as so many do in say, Rumba, and ensuring the students are "off-time" as a result.

And if an instructor ever intends to choreograph, then it is simply impossible to do so correctly without charting out the music. I am consistently stunned at the errors current "choreographers" have made because they did not chart the music, leading their students into utter chaos, confusion and failure.

No matter what, this knowledge is a must.

2. An instructor should know the basic patterns of the dance.

Too often basic patterns are only taught or shared in the context of footwork. For some students and classes this might be enough, such as group lessons for entertainment at weddings, or perhaps a free introduction course. But a trained instructor, who is expecting to teach such things as weekly classes or private lessons, should most certainly know more than just the general footwork.

First let me say that it is essential that any teacher should at least know the basics for both the leader and the follower, no matter what gender the teacher is. They don't have to know their counterparts' patterns and techniques as well as they do their own, but they should definitely know all of the following when it comes to their counterparts' basics.

A trained and worthwhile instructor should not only know the footwork of the leader and follower during all basic patterns, but also their accommodating center movements, frame and hand positions. For example, all teachers should know where the hands go, where the center faces and where the feet go during each beat of every basic pattern. Obviously such positions can be delved into with great detail when it comes to higher levels of training, but for most teachers, a basic understanding of where the hands should meet (in the hold of Waltz vs. the hold of WCS, etc), where the bodies should face, etc should be enough for most classes and students.

Of course, the higher the level of the student, the higher the quality of the instructor should be. Advanced instructors should definitely have a much deeper knowledge of the positions above. For example, I, as well as a few other master instructors in WCS, can break down hand positions literally to the exact bone in the finger of someone's hand. We can explain the 'whys' behind each position and advanced technique.

I should also mention here that when it comes to the specific training for each of the basics, the parts, done correctly, will strengthen and improve a person's body, not wear down, feel uncomfortable or strain anything on one's body. When I give a student a hand position, and they say they've been given another, I always ask them to dance a few basics with each technique, and decide for themselves which technique feels better on their body. I have yet to find a student that didn't chose my technique- and that is a reflection my skill, my background and my in depth training. I encourage all students and instructors, before training with someone they know little about, to first ask who they have trained with as well as who they currently train with.

A good instructor is always a student too.

If they do not have a chance to do so, I encourage them to always ask themselves after a lesson... "Does this feel really good on my body?" And adopt or drop the technique accordingly.

3. An instructor should know
the various calls that go with each pattern.

Some teachers only call a pattern in "quicks and slows." Some teachers only call a pattern by its numbers, or "count." Some teachers even swear by calling a pattern by the phrasing in the music. And others, in addition to numbers, only call in rolling count "& a 1 & a 2" or a straight count "& a 1 e & a 2 e."

For this reason, I believe all teachers should at least know about all of these calls, and what they mean. In my experience dancers look like stiff robots when they dance to a straight count call, but that's because I know the difference between a straight count and a rolling count. No matter what student I get, I can tell by their dancing which one they are doing. This is, of course, quite an advanced sort of eye, but still, I believe every teacher should at least be trained in the terminology, even if their eye is not developed.

It has also been my experience that, when teaching classes of about 100 students or so, 40-60% of the class will snatch up their Foxtrot or Rumba pattern when I call out the "count." Then I alternate to calling in "quicks and slows," and the other 60-40% instantaneously gets the pattern as well. After a while, I found myself consistently alternating between the two calls.

Most students do not notice at all, but it is always a purposeful choice on my part. If I call out 8 basics in a row of the Rumba, then I literally call out four of them using the "count" and four of them using quicks and slows. I alternating between the two at a rate that I find works for each particular class.

Sure, every once in a great while, I find a class in which 98% of the students respond only to the "count" call (engineers, anyone?) and sometimes I'll get the exact opposite. I never know, and therefore I never assume, and therefore I am prepared with an arsenal of tools and vocabulary that will work with no matter what kind of class I get.

And finally, when it comes to knowing the various calls, an instructor will be lost if they do not fully understand all of them and how they relate to one another. For example, every teacher should be prepared with the knowledge that a "quick quick" equals two weight changes during two beats of music and a "slow" means one weight change during two beats of music. And they should know how it's different with a Waltz, etc.

A teacher should know exactly what "count" that single weight change occurs on, etc. For example, when someone asks what the "count" is for a Country Two Step when the teacher has been calling "quicks and slows," then the teacher should be able to say that it's a 6 count pattern, and can call those counts in numbers as they dance, etc, etc.

Essentially, because there are so many ways of teaching out there, a true instructor should know what they all are, their differences and their relation to one another. I am not saying an instructor must absolutely teach in only one format, nor that they absolutely must teach in more than one, but I do believe that they must be trained in what all of them mean in relation to the basics of the dance they are teaching.

I certainly have my opinions on which produce better dancing, but that is for another article. For now, the vocabulary and the ability to switch between the calls of a dance's basics is quite enough.

4. An instructor should master the art of weight changes.

It is my honest and heartfelt opinion that any teacher who intends to charge for their lessons, especially private lessons, must have mastered the art of changing weight. In essence, I mean that they have mastered the ability to lead and follow with their centers, and not their arms.

This is perhaps the most difficult thing a teacher must learn to do, but it is essential. "Arm" leads & follows are almost always at the heart of partner dance injuries, along with hand holds (why I mention them in #2). There is no excuse for an instructor to put their students in harms way.

Yes, I'm saying that a teacher must be trained in "centering." In many ballrooms, instructors and students are trained to move their "core." In WCS, I was trained to narrow my body's center of movement down to the size of a golf ball in my solar plexus, whereas my friends who teach ballroom have narrowed their core down to the span of their ribcage.

Either one works for me when it comes to instructor training. If someone is leading by moving their "body"- i.e., their core, their solar plexus, their ribcage or their center... then they are usually using it to move their body's weight from one foot to another, allowing their frame to follow along.

Also, along with knowing the counts of the patterns I mention in points 2 and 3 above, a teacher must know that the counts and calls relate directly to weight changes. Again, if I call "quick, quick" in a Country Two Step, then I am aware that I am calling for two complete weight changes, occurring on counts "1" and "2" in the pattern, and often times, in order to help the class, the "1" and the "2" of the major phrase in the music.

All of these things... centering, weight changes, counts and calls... they relate to one another on almost every level. This is why it's so important that a trained instructor should understand them in regards to the dance they intend to teach.

5. An instructor should also know two other dances.

I know I'm going out on a limb here, but to be honest, this requirement comes as a result of the dancing and instruction that is inundating all partner dance communities today, especially West Coast Swing. 15 years ago, I never would have said that a teacher who wants to teach WCS would need to learn two other dances in order to be a good instructor.

But it is not 15 years ago. All partner dance communities, whether it be tango, ballroom or swing... they are all being affected by YouTube, TV Shows (*DWTS, SYTYCD, etc*) and the Millennial Generation. I talk about the cause & effects of these in great detail elsewhere, but for now, let's focus on the ever increasing results of these influences: 1. Dancers are no longer dancing "on beat" in many communities, 2. Dancers are unable to identify what music lends to what dance and 3. Dancers are increasingly dancing split weight.

In WCS, these three erosions are found worldwide. In other dances, such as tango, they are only occurring in certain cities or countries. But there are communities that seem much more "immune" to these three erosions... and all of those communities have one thing in common: the dancers in those communities all dance more than one dance.

Let's take Country Western for example. Country Western dancers are much more immune to Abstract Improvisation, a dance that is more on the Modern Dance side of things than a "lead & follow" partner dance. Why? Because CW dancers go to a dance and listen to every song that is played, and have to decide whether it is a Cha Cha, a Cowboy Cha Cha, a certain

Line Dance, a Two-Step or a Waltz, etc. To survive in their communities, they must know what music lends to what dance.

Not only that, but their music tends to be faster, requiring a higher level of lead and follow, and therefore they are more "immune" to the other two erosions- split weight and off time dancing. For example, if you dance a line dance and ignore the music, you will be completely run over in no time.

And that is why I believe all prospective instructors should learn two other dances. When a dancer knows more than one "lead and follow" dance, it "immunizes" them from the three common erosions. It prevents them from losing the character, the counts and the basic patterns of each dance once they start teaching, and helps them avoid the dangerous road of "do your own thing" no matter what the music or your partner is doing. I suppose if a teacher is being trained in ballroom, it is perhaps not as important to know another two dances, but it doesn't hurt, especially since erosions tend to spread like wildfire, especially with YouTube, etc.

But it is my absolute firm and resolved belief that anyone going into WCS, in the current climate, must absolutely know two other "lead and follow" dances. (I personally suggest one Latin and one Smooth, but that's just the educator in me.)

6. A prospective instructor will be able to identify Soft (Lyrical) Abstract Improvisation, Hard (Club) Abstract Improvisation and West Coast Swing when they see it and when they feel it in their partner.

Many local communities have already separated into their different dances... Abstract dancers go to one club and WCS dancers go to another. And this is good. This is healthy. They are two completely different dances with completely opposite goals, technique, mechanics and music. Abstract does not have basic patterns and it is not lead and follow and it is most certainly not centered.

Unfortunately, though, thousands of new dancers are going to YouTube to learn more about WCS, and Abstract Improvisation is almost all they will see and learn there instead. As such, if an instructor wants to teach WCS nowadays, especially if they live near a large city or have a demographic that is very much "plugged-in," aka, "online" all the time, then an instructor should know about all three dances and how they are danced, so that they are prepared when students ask questions or want to learn certain "things" they've seen online.

In California, where I live, most students are traveling to different dances with different instructors. As such, they are learning a variety of dances, Abstract, Zouk and Swing, all at the same time, and with everyone calling is WCS. They have been and are... utterly confused. And so, WCS teachers today, I believe, should be "in the know" when it comes to the dances out there on the floor.

And if you're a ballroom instructor? Well, I think you should know about what's going on in WCS too, because your dance might be next. Our "Abstract" instructors are waltzing their way in (no pun intended) to your studios worldwide. Sometimes your students see it for what it is right away... "Really? You want us to squat??? *Really????*" But not all students think for themselves or have as much training outside of WCS as you would think.

So in my opinion, anyone who teaches a partner dance should know what Abstract Improvisation is... because it's incredibly easy, incredibly deceptive and incredibly NOT in the bounds of any basic concepts held in any of the partner dances.

And there it all is. My basic requirements for prospective dance instructors. Of course, I certainly welcome students to learn and master all of the above as well. There is not one thing here that will not make you a better dancer, a greater success and a more powerful person. I wish you the best. And partner dancing really can feed your soul better than much in this world... but only when you learn it right, when you learn it well, when you learn what works....

From a truly trained instructor.

In Conclusion

This concludes all of the groundbreaking articles I have released to the public. Much has changed since the first one was released. I have loved hearing all the stories from the dancers they have impacted. It's been quite the adventure, the road from *The Nissy* to this book. And we're not quite done yet.

As mentioned earlier, I began writing *Weekly Notes* to my private email list in October of 2011. Now, exactly one year later, I'm compiling all of those notes into book format as well. It will be the first time every single note will be available to the public. I am doing my best to leave them un-edited, so that you may enjoy them just as my readers did, in order and untouched… the ups, the downs as well as the insides and outs! All of it will be laid bare.

You will watch me grow as a writer, probably even more so than you did here, and you will have some fun seeing what "all the fuss" was about when you heard about them through the grapevine, online, at events or in workshops.

Oh yes, it's been quite the ride. These articles changed the world of WCS and brought it from the edge of extinction. However, the *Weekly Notes* did a whole lot more than that. Oh, the stories I could tell! It will be fun sharing them with you, and I think you will really enjoy having the resource in your hands to reference and bookmark and travel while dancing.

And, as I've always said, I'm listening. Send me your stories, your experiences and your thoughts. I love hearing from my readers. I'm so glad you enjoy hearing from me as well.

Acknowledgements

This first journey from mind to pen to book was, for me, a long, hard and arduous one. I did not get here on my own. But I must first and foremost thank all of you that have shared your stories with me over the last 20 years. Without your questions, without your memories, without your trust, this book would never have been, nor would the discoveries it holds. Thank you.

To Dr. John Omaha, who unlocked the power within me to write, and who helped me discover my first article. To Larry Sonnenburg, who told me to go home and write. I did. To Rhonda Diamond, who said yes when I took my first step. To Josh Clark, who didn't leave, even when the going got tough.

To Harvey Bear, The Rancho Mirage Public Library and The Wright Brothers National Memorial – you got me here.

In memory of Tom Mattox, the director of my first convention, Cody Melin, who convinced me to stay, Wayne Bott, who taught me I could dance and finally, to Kenny Wetzel. You believed in me before anyone else.

To every reader who has written in who I cannot name here and to every student, studio and teacher who has remained faithful to swing, despite it all… you inspire me. Thank you.

And finally, to Jason, Julie, Kathryn, Dave & Ellen, James & Joella, Mark & Kim and so many more – thanks for going on this journey with us. We love you all so much.

What Readers Are Saying

The Articles

I wanted to let you know how much your articles meant to me after reading it... I started crying, literally. You put into words what I have felt for a long, long time... Thank you, again.
-Texas

… I further realize that I'm not alone with my questions. Thank you so much for giving us a voice and encouragement. It's nice to see that there are still dancers like you who dance truly from the heart.
-Canada

'The Time Has Come' explains exactly what is happening with West Coast Swing. I thought it was just a Perth dilemma, but it is actually international... Katherine puts it quite well.
-Australia

The Weekly Notes

I'm so glad to see someone getting these topics addressed in a forthright manner.
-Seattle

I really appreciate them.
There's so much information in one note...
-Finland

I'm inspired every time I read [them] - it's much to do with your craftsmanship of words - such wonderful and inspiring reading.
-California

Thank you so much for giving us a voice and encouragement.
-Canada

COMING SOON

Weekly WCS Notes: The Collection

ADDITIONAL RESOURCES

Katherine's Dance Website
www.wcskat.com

Katherine's Dance Blog
www.wcskat.blogspot.com

Katherine's YouTube Channel
www.youtube.com/GetSwingIN

15431451R00073

Made in the USA
Charleston, SC
02 November 2012